Not
as Far as
You Think

———

Not as Far as You Think

The Realities of Working Women

Lynda L. Moore

Lexington Books

D.C. Heath and Company/Lexington, Massachusetts/Toronto

Library of Congress Cataloging-in-Publication Data

Moore, Lynda L.
Not as far as you think.

Includes bibliographical references.
1. Women—Employment—United States—Addresses, essays, lectures.
2. Sex discrimination in employment—United States—Addresses, essays, lectures.
3. Women—United States—Psychology—Addresses, essays, lectures.
I. Title.
HD6095.M66   1986   331.4′ 0973   85-40109
ISBN 0-669-10836-7
ISBN 0-669-11945-8 (pbk.)

Published simultaneously in Canada
Printed in the United States of America
Casebound International Standard Book Number: 0-669-10836-7
Paperbound International Standard Book Number: 0-669-11945-8
Library of Congress Catalog Card Number: 85-40109

The paper used in this publication meets the minimum requirements of American National Standard for Information Sciences—Permanence of Paper for Printed Library Materials, ANSI Z39.48-1984.

The last numbers on the right below indicate the number and date of printing.

10 9 8 7 6 5 4 3 2

95 94 93 92 91 90 89 88 87 86

To Martin and Juliet

Contents

Acknowledgments

This book, like all major projects, began as an idea and would not have come into existence without the support and assistance of many people.

All the authors are to be commended for responding gracefully to the feedback and time lines that I gave them. Each has made a unique contribution, and yet all were committed to the overall purpose of the book.

The need for the book became apparent as a result of my professional experiences. In teaching, training, and consulting with women of all ages and careers, I discovered that although many opportunities exist, the barriers are still great for women in the workplace. This observation was reinforced by a national conference on women and organizations that I ran at Simmons College in 1984 and by my subsequent involvement in yearly research and programmatic conferences. I am grateful to the benefactor who, through Simmons College, recognized the importance of the concept and made it possible for me to complete this project. Both research findings and women's personal experiences attest to the gap between the popular image and the reality of working women's lives. This book attempts to address the very real problems that do still exist and offers some organizational and personal solutions in the hope that the gap between myth and reality will disappear.

Carol Davidson of The Wordworks performed masterfully the immense word processing task for the manuscript. Her skill and cheerfulness made the management of the technical logistics of the project not only possible but even pleasant.

My editor, Bruce Katz, played a crucial role in the development of this book—from believing in its importance to providing feedback on its content and structure. His personal and technical support were vital to the successful completion of the book.

Finally, I am thankful to all of my family, friends, and colleagues who supported me in this project and constantly reinforced its value and contribution toward creating an improved quality of work life for women and men and their organizations.

Not
as Far as
You Think

1
Introduction

Lynda L. Moore

The challenge now for women, as one writer puts it, isn't "getting in, it's getting on."[1] Women managers increase in numbers yearly, and the struggle to get women hired beyond entry level and into the corporate training program is being won. The crucial issue for women, many writers and observers agree, is the ability to rise beyond middle-management levels. Numbers don't tell the whole story: although we know that women are gaining access to entry-level management jobs, serious questions remain about the existence of real opportunities for women who have reached the lower levels of middle management. As many studies have shown, women still earn less than men, even with equivalent preparation and responsibilities. The so-called salary gap is objective evidence that sex discrimination still exists. One hope is that as increased numbers of women enter management, prejudice will disappear. But the problem, many women say, is that decisions about who rises to the top ranks tend to be more subjective than decisions dealing with lower- and middle-level jobs, and the older men who make those choices still don't feel comfortable with women. This is not considered overt discrimination; it is usually very subtle and often unconscious: those doing the choosing would never consider themselves to be discriminating against women. They are simply following their customary way of choosing people. However, top management positions are given to those who are perceived as trustworthy. Women at this level, as research has shown, tend to possess the same skills and characteristics as their male counterparts; the problems they are running into have to do with their *perceived* compatibility with top management—the comfort level of their "fit" with the top management team. Yet how can senior men learn to trust women as senior managers if there have never been any women to trust? It remains to be seen if increasing numbers of women will force the so-called glass ceiling for women to disappear as one of the final barriers to women's progress in organizations.

Not everyone agrees that there even *is* a problem for women. One writer recently claimed that attention to the so-called woman problem was myth-promoting and actually made it more difficult for women to succeed. Professional people, it is claimed, take their work seriously and don't have time to think about nonissues like the "woman issue." The belief that it really is tougher for women, this argument goes, creates a tendency for women to fall back on the myth as an excuse for nonproductivity.[2] Others claim it is not surprising that women have not yet been promoted to senior management: women haven't been in the work force long enough to have gained the experience for top management. Do women really face barriers? Or is it merely a function of time in the work force before we see women at top levels in all organizations?

This question is particularly pertinent for younger women. Women in their twenties tend to feel that the world has changed. Even if discrimination existed in the past, they believe things are different for women now. The women's movement has liberated women and allowed them to recognize the legitimacy of their career ambitions and their right to pursue roles other than housewife and mother or a sex-stereotyped "female" job. Affirmative action legislation has required organizations to give equal access to women and minorities in jobs and training programs. For the first time, schools and training programs have been opened to women so that they could be as well prepared as men to compete fairly on the basis of legitimate qualifications for the job. Training programs in schools and business made us all aware of the sexism deeply embedded in our culture and socialization. As men and women struggled to overcome the lessons of appropriate gender roles they had learned, new freedom and flexibility developed in both personal relationships and career opportunities. Today, women are expected to work and men to be supportive and to share equally in household and child-rearing activities. Employers are expected to give equal consideration to both working partners for relocation and promotion opportunities; child care is supported by the firm or, at the very least, is widely available at high quality and affordable cost.

Yet many women report that not until they are five or six years out of school do they realize that things are not as they expected. They see men with half their ability passing them by. They do not get much support, either financial or emotional, from employers and spouses for child care, maternity leave, and all the work-family conflict inherent in the situation of two professional people who are dedicated to their careers *and* trying to raise a family. They are shocked and disappointed. No one ever led them to believe that the work world would be like this—certainly not their professors, their parents, their friends. The media constantly portray them as superwomen, able to handle it all, seemingly with endless patience and energy and with eternal optimism that it *is* possible to have it all.

The problems women face vary according to their age, their career stage, their organization, and their industry; and different solutions are required. Yet there are some problems that all women face collectively, regardless of these factors, and these should concern us all. Only by understanding the problems all women face can we begin to sort out solutions and to appreciate the fact that although the problems may differ according to one's age or organization, the causes and results of those problems affect all women—and, ultimately, men and organizations as well.

Some believe that the problems women face are in fact created by the women themselves, not by men or their organizations. Women's psychological or internal barriers have received a lot of attention—lack of assertiveness, the so-called Cinderella complex, the superwoman syndrome, to name a few. In addition, some say the lack of appropriate training and experience is the reason women have not moved up. The real problems, this argument goes, are all a result of women not doing the right things to make themselves succeed.

Several chapters of this book address individual problems that women face and offer some solutions. In chapter 2 Landau and Amoss look at the issue of a woman's career and life stage and the specific problems that women face as a result of those factors. This chapter sets the tone for helping us understand and appreciate the problems women in general face specifically as a result of how old they are and how many years they have been working. They also address the disillusionment of younger women who enter the work force and find things are not as they expected.

The psychological impact of the presence of women in the work force has been widely discussed. There is an abundance of research and writing on the ways growing up female might hinder women. The definitive work on women in business, *The Managerial Woman*, pointed to women's lack of involvement in team sports, their reluctance to take risks, their self-doubt and identification with the nurturing and noncompetitive mother, and their tendency to rely on their own skills rather than to delegate and manage.

Lack of self-confidence is a theme that appears in several chapters in this book. The most central chapter dealing with this—the so-called imposter syndrome—is chapter 3 by Bell and Young. The phenomenon under investigation here is the feeling of self-doubt that plagues many women, often despite great achievement and demonstrated competency. The authors report on some of their research on the topic and relate their experiences in helping women overcome this troublesome and sometimes debilitating barrier, which prevents many women from pursuing an opportunity and, once found, from enjoying it.

A related self-concept issue for women is that of handling conflict and competition. Carol Gilligan in her research discovered that women perceive relationships as more important than winning at any cost and, as a result, have different approaches than men do to decision making and moral and ethical judgments. Gilligan's research has had a profound impact on our understanding of the psychology of women and their behavior at work. As a result of this socialization, women tend to approach conflict, negotiation, and competition differently than men do—not always to the women's benefit, as discussed in Kasten's chapter 8 on conflict and Greenhalgh and Gilkey's chapter 9 on negotiation. Some solutions are offered to help women better understand themselves and their strengths and weaknesses as they handle conflict, compete, and negotiate, all critical skills for not only survival but advancement.

Another aspect of women's behavior that has been widely written about and discussed is female-female relations and women's competitiveness with one another. Are women their own worst enemies? Why do some women say they would prefer to work for a man than for a woman? More often than not, the central issue seems to boil down to the way women relate to each other. Again, women in their twenties, as they enter organizations and careers, tend to expect other women (particularly higher up) to be particularly supportive—and are shocked when they aren't. Women have, in fact, been socialized to believe that they can't trust other women. One might expect that the feminist consciousness raising of the 1960s might have taught women to be supportive of each other. Instead, we see the queen bee syndrome—where an older woman, believing that a certain amount of dues must be paid, refuses to help a younger woman. This phenomenon has received a lot of attention, and many point to it as an example of how women create problems for themselves.

Another aspect of women's relationships is emerging as an important problem. Because older women are returning to the labor market, many younger women who have attended college or graduate school now supervise these older women. The particular problems that arise when traditional female authority roles are reversed have created a whole new set of manager-employee relations problems for both groups of women. In chapter 7, Henderson and Marple examine this problem and discuss how individual women and their companies might manage some of the supervisory issues arising from the situation.

Natasha Josefowitz in chapter 6 invites readers to consider how they can manage a variety of transitions in a career or an organization, given some of the behavioral issues that women bring with them into their lives at work. The particular problems of being a newcomer are discussed, whether you are a new employee or merely new to the department or to a job within a department.

We have discussed the internal or psychological problems women have at work. What kinds of external barriers do women face?

Many writers have claimed that women's lack of success has nothing to do with being women but is a result of the lack of support women face when they *do* attempt to achieve, particularly when they are married and have a family. Many consider the child care and dual career couple support issue a time bomb for the next generation of working women. Support from both company and spouse—emotional, financial, and logistical—is critical if a woman is to succeed. Hence the popular axiom that what every working woman needs is a wife. The so-called superwoman syndrome is much too high a price to pay for many women, who may be unwilling to make the trade-offs necessary in an attempt to juggle it all alone. In chapter 10, Beutell and Greenhaus discuss the work and family conflict that exists for all working couples and their companies, and suggest some strategies to resolve the conflict and create more satisfied *and* more productive people.

Research has shown that what women view as important but do not have in their organizations, and what they have but view as less important, shows a preference for substance over style.[3] Programs with more direct economic impact are preferred—cafeteria-style fringe benefits, career placement for a spouse, updated pension funding to accommodate women's longer life expectancy, and company-supported day care. All these programs represent the financial and logistical support women need to accommodate their multiple roles as breadwinners, spouses, and mothers. It has been said that women are afraid not of success, but of exhaustion. The lack of organizational and societal support does in fact lead to exhaustion for many women, which in turn fosters lowered ambitions and, in some cases, high turnover rates as women look for more supportive working environments. There is some speculation that the increasing number of entrepreneurial women is one result of women's disillusionment with the lack of all forms of organizational support.

Research has shown that women perceive a more progressive climate to exist in organizations that already employ a greater number of women. The idea is that if more women have worked in an organization, then formal policies and programs, as well as attitudes and behavior, will tend to be more favorable for women. This informal side of the organization, its *culture*, has received a lot of attention recently. Many popular books look at the importance of an organization's culture and tell managers how to create a culture with high productivity expectations. It seems important, then, to look at the culture of any organization in terms of how it responds to women and to *their* particular culture or needs.

A manager's style is very much influenced by the values of the organization's culture—the *tone* that top management sets. Lip service may be paid to developing and promoting women, but if real power and influence are never given to women, then the organization is not perceived as progressive for women, and individual women's productivity and satisfaction are blocked. Attitudes of bosses and co-workers alike determine the climate of an organization. Negative attitudes toward women or feelings of frustration among female managers are not conducive to a highly motivated and productive work life. Dissatisfaction can lead to turnover, a costly item for companies. The importance of these items to women's career satisfaction can be seen in articles listing the best companies for women to work for and even the best cities for women to work in—implying differences in regional attitudes toward women. Although company culture and reputation are of concern to men and women alike, these issues take on special significance for women, who need to assess a company's culture *specifically as it relates to women* in order to determine their chances of advancement in any particular firm or company.

Another issue of concern to women is sexual harassment. Books and articles abound which discuss the causes and solutions for this problem, from individual strategies to company policies and state and federal laws. Less has been written about the larger issue of the environment where men and women work together, and the natural attraction that occurs between men and women who interact on the jobs. As more men and women work together, particularly in positions of equal authority and power, attraction becomes a major issue. Recent writing in popular magazines suggests that there is increasing attention to this phenomenon. Spelman et al. in chapter 5 help us to understand how and why attraction develops on the job, and how organizational culture and climate can foster its development. We all need to be aware of the potential for attraction to develop in order to decide how to handle the complex situations that can arise on the job as a result. It is particularly important for women to pay attention to this issue since, unfortunately, as with sexual harassment, they bear the negative consequences more often than men.

Managing the culture of the organization is the theme of chapter 4 by Keele. *Mentoring* and *networking* are often discussed as examples of political skills, part of the game women have never learned to play and need to learn in order to survive in organizations and, particularly, to advance. Understanding power and recognizing the need to build power bases and establish alliances and influence are considered crucial skills for success. Mary Cunningham has identified one of the reasons for her downfall (and her mentor's) at Bendix as her lack of recognition of the power structure of the organization and of the need to build strong alliances, particularly if one has climbed quickly to a position of power. Managing peer and boss relationships, then, can be as crucial as managing subordinates in a supervisory or managerial role. Even at other levels, different kinds of relationships must be cultivated to meet both career information and personal social needs on the job. In chapter 4, Keele gives us some insight into the types of relationships we need and why they are important for individual women and their companies to ensure effectiveness at work.

A great deal has been written about the new management styles calling for more participative forms of management: theory Z, Japanese management, quality circles. Some of the more popular books on the subject—*In Search of Excellence*; its sequel, *Passion for Excellence*; and *The Change Masters*—argue that companies can remain competitive only by managing with a more person-centered, creative, and caring approach. Research has shown that companies where creativity, autonomy, good communication, and sensitivity to employees are emphasized produce high-performing firms and satisfied employees.

These characteristics, now being cited as necessary for high productivity and satisfaction, are in fact traditionally feminine behaviors. Women, then, are getting contradictory advice. Popular books and articles tell women to learn to play the game, to adapt to the male culture of organizations, to become less sensitive and more bottom-line oriented, to be less concerned with process and more with getting the job done. In chapter 11 Mark Lipton argues that management *is* still masculine in nature and that the cloning effect of managerial selection continually leaves women out of the picture. Managerial androgyny, whereby female managers would incorporate both male and female behaviors, is a myth, Lipton argues. The real issue is not competence, but perceived comfort with the difference between men and women, that blocks women's career advancement.

If in fact organizational cultures are changing, then women are caught in another Catch-22 situation: they are told to change their behavior to adapt to organizational cultures, only to find that at certain levels (or in certain organizations), those very behaviors harm them more than help them.

In the final chapter, Rosabeth Moss Kanter discusses another element of managing an organization's environment or culture: the skills necessary to influence and innovate, rather than the skills needed to play political survival games. Playing political games, Kanter says, was important when competition was less stiff and more industries and organizations were stable. In today's increasingly competitive environment, however, organizations are concerned with survival; the women who advance will be those who solve key organizational problems and who influence others to take risks and to innovate in order for the firm to remain competitive. Reading the environment, then, requires the ability to see what is needed for advancement as it relates to organizational survival and development.

The barriers women face, then, are both internal and external. The issues discussed in this book are diverse and far-ranging. I hope these chapters will force us all to think critically about the nature of working women's problems and the gap between the media portrayal and the reality of working women's lives. It is a confusing time for women and men: for women, the opportunities before them go beyond their mothers' wildest dreams, yet although some of their struggles have long histories, others have no precedent. The reality of working women's lives is a story of change, both individual and organizational. Men and organizations respond with both accommodation and resistance. Accommodation here can be viewed not as change or adaptation but merely as a more subtle form of resistance.

Contrary to their media image, women have not climbed as far as their male counterparts, and they still face considerable problems. Despite a decade of affirmative action, many problems still need to be resolved before women can not just enter organizational hierarchies but also compete and advance along with their male counterparts.

The diagnosis of any problem suggests its cure: let's not blame the victim but, rather, look at all levels of responsibility in analyzing and solving problems. The problems are both internal and external in nature; they call for individual male and female changes, and for institutional and organizational changes as well. Many problems that women face need much more analysis and research before we can run the risk of implementing easy solutions. The solutions offered for the problems discussed here are both individual and organizational and suggest the need to understand women's problems from both perspectives.

Organizations and their managers need to understand that developing programs that go beyond token responses is, in the long run, less expensive than potential lawsuits and the waste of underutilized talent. If, as many have claimed, industry's biggest future problem will be a shortage of capable people at all levels, then managers can no longer afford to ignore half the population when they are seeking talented employees. Organizations that want to recruit and retain well-qualified women and utilize them to their fullest extent will have to pay much more attention to their programs, policies, and overall culture as these environmental factors serve to encourage the development of women in all functions and levels.

There are social and moral as well as economic reasons to seek solutions to the problems addressed here. These reasons must be accepted before any person—male or female—or any organization is likely to change.

Notes

1. Felice N. Schwartz, "From Getting In to Getting On," *Working Woman*, September 1983, pp. 131–133.
2. Geraldine Spruell, "Making It, Big Time—Is It Really Tougher for Women?" *Training and Development Journal*, August 1985, pp. 30–33.
3. Warren Boeker, Rebecca Blair, M. Frances Van Loo, and Karlene Roberts, "Are the Expectations of Women Managers Being Met?" *California Management Review* 27, no. 3 (Spring 1985):148–157.

References

Bernikow, Louise. 1984. "We're Dancing As Fast As We Can." *Savvy*, April, pp. 40–44.
Businessweek. 1984. "You've Come a Long Way, Baby—But Not as Far as You Thought." *Businessweek*, October 1, pp. 126–131.

Frank, Susan. 1984. "Why Women Aren't Getting to the Top." *Fortune*, April 16, pp. 40–45.

Gilligan, Carol. 1983. *In a Different Voice: Psychological Theory and Women's Development*. Cambridge, Mass.: Harvard University Press.

Hall, Jennifer Bingham. 1982. "Female Bosses Say Biggest Barriers Are Insecurity and 'Being a Woman'," *Wall Street Journal*, November 2, pp. 31–32.

Hennig, Margaret, and Jardin, Anne. 1977. *The Managerial Woman*. New York: Anchor Press/Doubleday.

Kanter, Rosabeth Moss. 1983. *The Change Masters*. New York: Simon and Schuster.

Peters, Thomas J., and Waterman, Robert H., Jr. 1982. *In Search of Excellence: Lessons from America's Best-Run Companies*. New York: Harper and Row.

Rogan, Helen. 1984. Series of articles, Report of a Wall Street Journal/Gallup Survey on Female Executives, *The Wall Street Journal*, week of October 29.

Safran, Claire. 1984. "Corporate Women: Just How Far Have We Come?" *Working Woman*, March, pp. 99–104.

2

Myths, Dreams, and Disappointments: Preparing Women for the Future

Jacqueline Landau
Lisa Amoss

Where do I expect to be ten years from now? Well, I'd like to be vice-president of a small company. I'll work hard, and hopefully will be promoted every year. Once I start to establish myself, in about five years or so, I'd like to get married and have a couple of kids.

This is a typical comment we, as educators, hear from twenty-one-year-old female business school students. Close to 50 percent of business school students are women. These women embark on their careers with great confidence and enthusiasm, often convinced that discrimination is a problem of the past. They expect to be offered challenging and exciting jobs that provide rapid advancement and high salaries. As they climb the corporate ladder, they plan to meet the men of their dreams, who will be supportive of their careers and share equally in household and child care responsibilities.

How realistic is this scenario? Can women have it all? Are they rising rapidly to the top of the corporate ladder? Are they meeting men who are supportive of their corporate ascent? Will their high expectations be met? To answer these questions, we sent out a survey to 1,200 alumni of a medium-sized business school, most of them between the ages of twenty-one and thirty-five. In this chapter

The authors gratefully acknowledge the contribution of Pat Somers and Christine Lentz to the development of this chapter.

we discuss the results of this survey—results that were sometimes surprising, sometimes predictable, yet always thought-provoking.

Are Women Getting Ahead as Quickly as Men?

I invested two years of my life in getting an MBA. After graduation, I got a good job with a great, prestigious company. I've done well for five years, gotten promotions, played all the games. Now I look around and ask myself: Where am I going? I seem to be getting stuck. I don't see the big rewards coming. And I'm not even completely sure whether I really want those big rewards. Am I successful? . . . I'm not certain I really know what success is!

This kind of grumbling is frequently heard from professional women who have, in the past ten years, chosen careers in business. These women did well in business school, often graduating at the top of their classes. Their technical skills were excellent, and they were rewarded with excellent initial job offers. Their starting salaries were comparable to those of their male counterparts. They worked hard and at first were promoted as rapidly as their male colleagues. Our survey results showed, however, that this equity remained only for the first two or three years. Then the men began outpacing women, particularly in terms of salary. In our study, of those alumni who had been out of school five years or less, 60 percent of the women but only 40 percent of the men were earning less than $30,000 a year. Fourteen percent of the men but only 5 percent of the women were making over $50,000. The differences in salary remained even when taking into account the number of years of work experience, the type of degree (undergraduate or MBA), and the type of organization the individual worked for.

These statistics have been corroborated on a national level. Jaret Jones-Parker, executive director of the Association of Executive Search Consultants, reports in a *Fortune* article, "Why Women Aren't Getting to the Top," "After eight or ten years, [women] hit a barrier. . . . There is an invisible ceiling for women at that level." At a point where men are beginning to make their bids for the top, women are getting stuck. The number of places at the top is small, and the factors that contribute to success become harder to define. Women have invested a lot in their careers, but the big payoffs are proving elusive. These women are technically as well prepared for their careers as the men they work with; they have the degrees, the grades, and the experience. What factors are causing the differences in their long-term success?

Success: What Is It?

In answering that question, perhaps the place to start is with the definition of success. Traditionally, success in business has been measured in terms of dollars: those who make the most money are the most successful. Most of us look at material possessions to determine whether or not people are successful. Successful people are the ones who drive the Mercedes, who live in the big houses, who wear expensive suits. We have some reason to believe, however, that men and women in business define success in different ways. When asked to paint a picture of success, many men will instantly say something like "Vice-president by age forty, making $150,000 a year." There isn't much doubt in their minds. Women, on the other hand, are not quite so sure, especially after a few years in the work world. For them, success can mean any of several different kinds of things. They find it harder to separate their careers from other, more personal parts of their lives. Is success measured by salary, by working conditions, or by the people you work with? More women than men are unclear.

One explanation is that it is more difficult for women to have both successful careers and personal lives. Success in one area hinders success in the other. We asked women whether their careers had any significant impact on their long-range decisions about their personal lives:

> Family life is more important than a career. When I have children, I will stop working.

> I delayed having children because of the time and pressure of my career.

> I am postponing getting married.

> I decided I'd rather be single than with an unsupportive, uncommitted partner, so I broke off a long-term relationship recently. My career demands are paramount now, but I resent them and I am fighting to maintain some of my own time.

Men on the other hand, saw career success as enabling them to do what they wanted.

> My career has enabled me to be financially stable, so I could start a family without worrying about money.
>
> My career has given me money, security, and upward promotions, so I can have the kind of personal life I want.

Some men complained that their careers prevented them from spending as much time with their families as they would like, but they were more likely than women to have families. Sixty percent of the men but only 40 percent of the women who answered our survey were married.

Given the comments we have heard from alumni, it is not surprising that women are more ambivalent about what success is. They start off defining success in terms of career advancement and money, but by the time they reach age twenty-five and have found that they have had to compromise in their personal lives, their definition of success may begin to change. To discover why women are having this problem defining success, we looked at what they expected from a job and from personal relationships and compared this to what they were getting. We also asked them whether they were planning for their future.

What Do Women Want from a Job?

Women tend to expect more from a job than their male counterparts do. They stated that they want jobs with pleasant working conditions, friendly co-workers and supervisors they admire and respect. They also want jobs that are intellectually stimulating and respected by other people, and that enable them to develop their knowledge and skills. Men also want jobs with these characteristics, but these factors are less important to them. As men gain work experience, their expectations about what a job can provide decrease. Women, however, remain eternally optimistic. Their chances of being disappointed are greater because their expectations are too high. When they don't get what they want, they begin to question the time and effort they put into their careers at the expense of their personal lives. Some even decide to drop out of the work force.

As Ann, who has both an MBA and a Masters degree in Hospital Administration, put it:

> I used to think I'd define myself in terms of my work. But now [after four years] I find I want to plan my *life* rather than a career. I am no longer working for pay.

Career Planning: Men Do It, Women Don't

Do you plan your career or leave it pretty much to chance? When asked whether they have a definite plan for the next five years, more men than women answer "yes." Women, particularly if they are between the ages of twenty-five and thirty, tend to say they have a vague plan or they're not sure. Many men in business have plotted out their next moves and are aware of which moves will lead where. The more work experience they have, the more career planning they do. They are not focused too heavily on their present job, but tend to see it as a means of getting somewhere else. This probably allows them a certain amount of risk-taking. Although this risk-taking can lead to problems, it can also lead to great success.

In one large multinational firm, young professionals are transferred every eighteen to twenty-four months. They are rotated around the organization so that they can have broad exposure and a variety of learning opportunities. Those who make a strong impact on the job within that short eighteen- to twenty-four month period are the ones who are noticed and rewarded. But making an impact under these conditions often requires taking considerable risk: one must act quickly, go out on a limb, do something different. The long-term implications of some of these risky actions can be very damaging to the organization, but the full implications may not show up for quite a while. By the time they do, the young professional who made the initial decision is often long gone. He has been rewarded for being creative, saving money, taking a definite action—and he's gone on to the next step in his career plan. The final results rarely catch up to him!

One young turk (as the high-flyers in this company are known) decided to change a long-established way of doing business in his department in order to tighten up on materials costs. He acted with-

out consulting the older supervisors who had been in the department a long time. For the next few months, the department budget
looked great. Costs were down, profits were up. The young man
was promoted; indeed, he was moved to a facility in another city.
Six months later, machinery started breaking down in this former
department. Only the older supervisors who remained realized that
his procedural change was at fault.

Women tend to be much more uncomfortable in this type of system than men. Their focus is more on doing a good, thorough job
now than it is on the next job down the line. They are more likely,
after several line assignments, to request transfer to a staff position—
one that will be safer and less risky, but will also effectively stop the
upward progression of their career in this organization.

It's legitimate to ask why women, particularly those between
twenty-five and thirty, are less likely to plan for career success than
men. There are several factors involved. Women as a group tend to
believe that their lives are controlled by factors outside their own
control. This tendency has been substantiated over and over by research.[1] Women are more likely to attribute their career success to
luck. They are more likely to believe that what happens to them is
controlled by others: their boss, their husband, their family. How
often do we hear a woman who has been complimented on a promotion answer, "Yes, I was lucky!"

Women do less planning because, either consciously or subcon-
sciously, they don't believe that planning will make any difference.
Whatever is going to happen to them will happen no matter what they
do. Even women in our 1984 study of business professionals indicated
that they felt this way. When asked to list factors that contribute to
career success, they often mentioned "luck," "the ability to deal with
people," "the ability to listen"—all factors concerned with other people
and what will happen to the women through others. In contrast, men
are likely to identify "being aggressive" and "recognizing opportunities
and going after them" as factors in their career success.

Women may also do less planning because they really do have
less control over their lives. Their spouses may not be as supportive as
they would like. Their children may make more demands on their
time than they expected. By age twenty-five they may realize that
plans can quickly evaporate if they want to start or maintain a family.

Can Women Have a Rewarding Family Life and a Successful Top-Level Career, Too?

As we have already demonstrated, it is still quite likely that the answer to this question will be "yes" for men and "no" for women. One reason is that women are still much more likely than men to feel and take ultimate responsibility for the management of their families. A major study of couples in the United States, completed in 1983, found that the majority of men were "work-centered" whereas the majority of women were "relationship-centered."[2] This is true no matter what the woman's field or level in an organization. Although most women now work outside the home, even when they have small children, they never really give up responsibility for being custodians of the family. This tends to place a double burden on them when they are striving for both career and family success. Their time and energy are drained; their loyalties are divided.

Mary Anne Devanna, in her study of Columbia Business School graduates in 1980, found a big difference in the salaries ultimately achieved by men and women. She heard a recurring theme: women don't take their careers seriously. Fears that women would leave to have a family were common, and women with small children themselves reported markedly increased pressures. Indeed, many women appear to have chosen not to marry or not to have children rather than face these pressures. Most organizations have not addressed these issues in any meaningful way.

Any woman who attends professional association meetings in her field with other women knows that a considerable amount of conversation revolves around juggling career and family obligations. This is certainly not true among men in similar settings. Many men today are performing more household tasks than men did in the past, but they do not take a primary responsibility for managing their relationships and family lives, nor is that responsibility split equally. In the vast majority of cases, it falls to women.

In our survey, we found that men still have very traditional ideas about relationships. They were less likely than women to believe that household tasks such as washing dishes, preparing meals, and doing laundry should be divided equally. They were also less likely to believe that if both partners work full time, both careers should be considered equally in deciding where they will live. Women believed that both partners in a relationship should share the responsibility for making important decisions, whereas men were more likely to believe the male partner should have the final say.

Men were more likely than women to think that two partners in a relationship should pool all their property and financial assets, and that when there are small children in the home, it would be better for the mother not to work. Men were also more likely to agree with the idea that a member of a couple who have been together a long time should not accept a job in a distant city if it means ending the relationship.

Women thought that both they and their partners shared in making decisions affecting their relationship. Men were more likely to state that they (the man) should and did have more say. Women tended to say that both they and their partner were equally committed to the relationship, whereas men had a tendency to believe that the female partner was more committed.

Women tended to believe that they have altered their habits and ways of doing things more than their partner has, in order to please their partner. Men agreed that the female in the relationship was more likely to change habits to accommodate the relationship.

A Question of Commitment

Ask any employer what qualities are desirable in an employee—*commitment* will appear at or near the top of the list. Strong commitment is necessary from anyone who wants a successful career.

Commitment is also necessary in a relationship. The ability to believe in and be strongly supportive of the other person is often the glue that holds a couple or a family together, especially in trying times. The stronger the commitment, the more successful the relationship is likely to be.

Now research is showing that commitment is a particularly necessary element in dual-career relationships. Hall and Hall have found that mutual commitment to the career of the other is a powerful determinant of success.[3] Each member of the couple must be strongly committed to the other's career. This deep commitment will help to carry the couple through the inevitable conflicting pri-

orities, disagreements, and disappointments that will sometimes occur as they attempt to combine two careers with a personal relationship. It will help keep the lines of communication open in both good
and bad times. It will provide a base for resolving both large-scale
problems, like deciding where to move when one has a career opportunity, and small everyday questions, like who cooks or shops or
cares for children.

But Ann's statement, "He considers his career more important,"
is frequently heard from women who are involved in dual-career
relationships. When asked who is more committed to the career of
the other, both men and women tend to answer that the woman is
more committed to the man's career than he is to hers. It is typical
for the woman in such a relationship to make more adjustments to
fit the man's career needs. This can be a problem for the woman
who is trying for career success. It means that she must be strongly
committed both to her own career and to that of her partner, but
cannot expect him to be equally committed to her career. Often her
own career success suffers.

So Where Are Professional Women Now?

The female business school graduate starts out with high hopes and
expectations. She has the same skills and ambitions as her male colleagues, the same determination to have a successful career. She
often finds, however, that she can have a successful career only at
the expense of her personal life. By the age of twenty-five, she may
begin to question her definition of success and her devotion to her
career. At the same age, her male counterpart is solidifying his career plans as he works his way up the corporate ladder.

The female business school graduate wonders where and when
she will find the supportive spouse she is looking for. If she is
already married, unless she is very lucky, she may be coming to the
realization that most of the compromises in the relationship are likely to be hers. She is trying to figure out how she can have children
and still retain her career momentum. These are all issues that may
not have seriously concerned her when she was twenty. Now, unprepared for what lies ahead, she faces disillusionment, disappointment, and a feeling that she no longer has control over her life.

Some women choose to leave the corporation and go into business for themselves in search of more control and greater flexibility.

Of course, this does not happen to all women. Some, like the so-called Young Achievers described recently in a Wall Street Journal/Gallup survey of female executives, are reaching the upper corporate echelons, and are either happy being single or have found supportive spouses. They manage to have satisfying career and personal lives simultaneously. If women were better prepared for the problems and issues they may face in the future, perhaps more of them would be able to have the successful careers and personal lives they envisioned as young adults.

Are There Any Answers?

We do not believe the situation is hopeless. Women can be better prepared for the conflicts they will face. They can be taught to have more realistic expectations about their careers and personal lives. First, colleges and universities should provide information to students early in their college experience. The best information comes from people working in business or other professions. Activities like career days where alumni/alumnae participate in panel discussions are particularly effective.

Second, students could be matched with alumni and alumnae on an ongoing basis to talk about career issues. When describing her experience in business school, Laura, a financial analyst, said: "Each student had to reinvent the wheel. There was a need for information . . . maybe a mentor series where women alumnae would come back and talk about their experience." Martha felt that a refresher course for women addressing their special needs would be helpful. As Ann commented, "Until you're aware it's a problem, you don't really listen." Many business school students, both male and female, don't know what to expect.

Experiential learning can also help students become more realistic. This can include class projects, observation experiences, internships, part-time jobs, and summer jobs. The more experience a student has, the more realistic his or her career and life goals will be.

Organizations that employ new college graduates could work more closely with colleges and universities in facilitating the career planning of students. Students who have unrealistic expectations will never be satisfied, productive employees. They may become quickly disillusioned with work, and may leave the organization or produce only what is absolutely necessary in order to retain their jobs. Stress due to conflicts between career and personal lives also may take its toll at the workplace if people are unprepared to deal with these conflicts. Organizations must place a greater emphasis on conveying to faculty, as well as to college placement offices, the importance of realistic expectations, and must aid faculty and placement directors by encouraging their employees to participate in career days, classes, and internship programs.

Final Words of Advice

What final words of advice would we give to young women embarking on business and professional careers today? First, we would tell them to focus and narrow their expectations of jobs and careers and to be more aware of what is realistic and what actually can be provided. In order to do this, they need to see themselves as controlling their own destinies, and to act in ways that will help them take control rather than relying on others. Also, women need to engage in realistic long-term career planning, to plot out possibilities for their careers and then take actions to make those possibilities materialize. This should include conscious goal-setting and priority-setting, and good knowledge of what is available to them. They need to be *proactive* toward their careers—to make things happen.

If women are to attain career success without sacrificing family life, both men and women will need to shift their orientation to one that is concurrently relationship-centered and work-centered, and will allow both partners to focus attention on these two critically important areas. Each partner must be strongly committed to their relationship and to both careers.

Finally, we would tell women to realize that compromises will be necessary, both at home and at work. As Mark, a thirty-three-year-old man who makes over $70,000 a year as president of a company, stated: "With each partner having specific interests, neither of us has paid attention to the needs and wants of the other. This has become quite a problem, and we are both unhappy, although we both have 'successful' careers."

What women must remember, however, is that they do not have to make all the compromises. Nor should they abandon their plans because things don't turn out exactly as they once expected.

Notes

1. K. Deaux and T. Emswiller, "Explanations of Successful Performance on Sex-linked Tasks: What Is Skill for the Male Is Luck for the Female," *Journal of Personality and Social Psychology 19* (1974):80–85.
2. R. Rapoport and R. Rapoport, *Working Couples* (New York: Harper & Row, 1978).
3. F.S. Hall and D.T. Hall, *The Two-Career Couple* (Reading, Mass.: Addison-Wesley, 1979).

References

Devanna, Maryanne, 1984. "Male/Female Careers First Decade: A Study of MBA's." New York: The Center for Research in Career Development, Columbia University Graduate School of Business.

3

Imposters, Fakes, and Frauds

Lee Bell
Valerie Young

Imposters, Fakes, and Frauds: Competence and Confidence in the Workplace" is the title we have given to a career-related workshop developed in response to the surprisingly vast number of bright and capable women who, despite external evidence to the contrary, continue to doubt their competence. By downplaying or dismissing their abilities and accomplishments, such women are often stymied in their careers. They operate with the disabling belief that they are, in effect, imposters or fakes or frauds.

We began to conduct workshops to talk about these issues with other women, to share our research, and to provide support and concrete strategies to counteract this syndrome. The response to our attempt to address women's feelings of fraudulence systematically was instantaneous and overwhelming. Over the past few years hundreds of women from all walks of life have attended the seminar—engineers, realtors, so-called displaced homemakers, college professors, artists, nurses, computer analysts, and lawyers, to name a few.

This debilitating syndrome, compounded by the ever-present fear of being unmasked, interferes with women's productivity, effectiveness, and advancement potential. The cost to organizations in terms of unrealized potential could be enormous and should be a concern to managers who need to develop fully the human resources available to them.

We also recognized that although men often share feelings of imposterism, women suffer from this syndrome with greater frequency. Sociocultural expectations and realities contribute to making women feel like imposters in ways that men don't. The sex-role expectations of our culture, for example, frequently impair women's sense of themselves as valuable and permanent members of the work force. In addition, women must endure in a male-oriented and male-defined work world, where their worth is often depreciated.

Interrupting the imposter syndrome necessitates collective as well as personal strategies for breaking both the psychological barriers that prevent women from experiencing their own competence and the social barriers that reinforce the psychological ones.

Our work here will focus on women's internal psychological barriers. First, we will examine the ways in which women dismiss proof of their abilities and the various sources of fraudulent feelings. Next we will describe a step by step process that has proved effective in helping individuals to assess the self-limiting patterns that undermine them in their work lives. Finally, we will suggest concrete strategies for both individual and organizational change.

As much as possible, we will let the women we have worked with speak for themselves. Our work originates from three sources. The first is relevant research on women and achievement. Foremost will be interviews conducted by one of the authors to discover the kind of internal barriers undermining women's occupational achievement. The women interviewed were university professors and administrators, training consultants and management development specialists, and career counselors. They were asked to share their observations about the kinds of self-inhibiting attitudes and behaviors blocking women in their work lives. Their combined experiences and insights shed considerable light on some of the reasons that women might feel like imposters. Unless otherwise noted, all quotes are those of the various interviewees.

Second, we will be offering anecdotal evidence gleaned from our experience conducting the "Imposters, Fakes and Frauds" seminar. Finally, our work emanates from our own very personal experience as "recovering imposters"—a term we use to underscore the ongoing process involved in unlearning the deep-seated feelings of fraudulence.

What Is an Imposter?

In their clinical work with high-achieving, successful women, Pauline Clance and Suzanne Imes found that regardless of impressive personal accomplishments—academic distinction, status, recognition, and professional advancement—the vast majority of their clients did not internalize their successes. Instead, their clients perceived themselves to be "imposters" who had somehow managed to slip through the system undetected.[1]

The imposter syndrome is not limited to high-achieving women or to women in nontraditional fields, as evidenced by the number of nurses, teachers, and human service providers attending our seminars. What distinguishes imposters is a pattern of acknowledged competence, on the one hand, and self-doubt and negative-evaluation on the other. Such women have a strong fear of being exposed as intellectual frauds.

One way that self-defined imposters reconcile this contradictory self-image is by ignoring evidence that confirms their competence. The women interviewed were all too familiar with the self-negating practices of women. "It has astonished me," reported a therapist specializing in women's achievement-related blocks, "to encounter women who are clearly intelligent, competent, and capable and have them be so completely able to push that away." For such women, she added, "confidence doesn't accumulate; only negative evidence weighs on the scale—positive evidence weighs nothing." Because women are reported to be particularly hard on and unforgiving of themselves, they are more apt to ignore the positive evaluations they receive from others. According to one management training specialist, "our internal eye is just very critical, and so when the internal eye's examination doesn't match up to the external feedback—we suspect the external feedback."

In contrast, when a man fails, even on a task requiring skill, he is more apt to attribute failure to external factors such as "bad luck."[2] Women are frequently unable to take pride in their own accomplishments because they attribute failure to internal factors and success to external ones.[3] This is evident in the comments made by a program counselor at a technical training school for women:

> The successes are not fully internalized—meaning, women don't often take credit for what they've done. So that in a situation where they may have a responsible job, it's emotionally unclear how they got there. If I experience myself to be this complete failure then I can't accept the credit for the successes that I don't even see and that I don't recognize as mine.

Sources of Fraudulent Feelings

How do fully competent, intelligent women come to explain away their own hard-won achievements? What causes obviously bright and capable individuals to believe they are merely faking their way through the world of work? The answers have been traced to three sources: (1) early messages and expectations; (2) the male-oriented nature of the work world; and (3) women's definition of competence, success, and failure.

Early Messages and Expectations

Achievement for females is often valued in the abstract. In our own families, the majority of participants reported that they were encouraged and indeed expected to go to college. Attending college, however, was frequently an end in and of itself, rather than a step *toward* something else. With rare exception, women say they can't remember being encouraged to *do* anything with their degree. They were expected merely to because a well-rounded individual who, presumably, could then attract a future mate who *was* expected to utilize his training.

On a similar note, Nancy Chodorow asserts that most girls receive conflicting and competing messages about future roles. Schooling for females, she says, is really a "pseudotraining" that is "not meant to interfere with the much more important training to be 'feminine' and a wife and mother, which is embedded in the girl's unconscious development."[4] Well-intended parental messages ("Go to college so you'll have something to fall back on if something happens to your husband") can have the effect of undercutting a woman's sense of herself as a future full-time member of the work force.

Although many women do not expect work to be central in their lives, for most it turns out to be so. Thus one reason why adult women might feel like imposters is that they never envisioned themselves out in the work world. When past expectations clash with present reality, the result can be a sense that one is not a legitimate member of the work community. A management-training specialist recounts a telling example of this conflict. A woman in her company disclosed that even after finishing college she continued to picture herself becoming a homemaker and mother, married to a successful man who would provide all of the income. She did marry but was soon widowed. When she was forced to get an entry-level job to support herself, her intelligence and hard work reaped her promotion after promotion. Surprised at each advancement, she feared that the promotion would only be temporary. Her career advanced rapidly; yet she remains haunted by this sense of occupational illegitimacy. Recounts the training specialist:

> Now she's 47, she's the vice-president and she can't believe that this is real . . . that this is her life. . . . She says, "I wake up and I look at myself in the mirror and I say—*who are you*?! This is not what you are supposed to be. You're not supposed to go to work and be head of a large department; you're supposed to stay home, and type, and do work for the church, and take care of the kids, and wait till hubby comes home. What are you doing?" Success came as an amazement to her.[5]

The Male-Oriented Work World

Women from all racial and socioeconomic groups share the often alienating experience of having to compete in a work world dominated by white men. In a perverse way there may be some validity to feelings of imposterism because women have not been a part of what one subject called the "success circle." As one nationally known consultant put it:

> The system of business in corporate America was designed by men and according to male values, so in a real sense we are fakes because the system was not designed for us. Not having a history of belonging makes one feel like an imposter.

The way women as a class are treated in the work world also seems to foster insecurity. Another prominent workshop leader points out that the devaluation of so-called women's work evident in hiring, salary, and promotion inequities simply "reinforces women's perception that they are not valuable people, that they're not competent, that they're not doing work that is essential." Apart from the larger system, which as a whole exploits, disempowers, and discriminates against its female work force, women's self-doubts are further compounded by the attitudes and behaviors of individual men they encounter daily. Their male colleagues regularly interrupt, exclude, invalidate, stereotype, trivialize, and protect them; and in all of this the self-doubting woman reads a message that powerfully reinforces her own negative self-image.

Finally, one educator linked women's anxiety about failure and making mistakes to a tendency of others to "magnify women's mistakes and sell them as proof of women's lack of qualifications." In other words, when a woman succeeds, she succeeds on her own, an individual, an oddity—or so it is believed. But when she fails, she fails as a representative of her sex. This pressure becomes heightened for black, Latina, Asian and Native American women, who often are expected to excel as representatives of both their race and their sex. Similarly, a blind workshop participant was distressed that if she didn't "cut it" at her new job, then future disabled applicants would be told, "I'm sorry, but we tried one of you people and it didn't work out."

Competence, Failure, and Success Female-Style

Women's early messages and expectations and later experiences in the male-oriented work world are not the only sources of fraudulent feelings. Our research identifies three interconnected areas as crucial to our understanding of the internal barriers impeding women: competence, failure, and success. Because of their significance to the topic at hand, they will be addressed in some detail.

*Com•pe•tence \ n   1.: perfection   2.: expertise
3: unassisted achievement   4: unattainable*

Most women tend to share a definition of competence guided by standards that are unnecessarily high. For many women, competence is equated with flawless performance. "Competence is seen as perfectionism," stated one career counselor. "The assumption is that performing competently means that you've got it down pat and that there is no room for fluctuation or . . . different levels of competence.

Before applying for a new position, for example, many women assume they need to know 150 percent of what it takes to carry out the new job. In *Games Mother Never Taught You*, Betty Lehan Harragan observes that men are more likely to feel qualified if they possess a mere 40 percent of the skills and knowledge required for the new position. Men know that in a majority of occupations it is expected that the candidate will learn the remaining 60 percent *on the job.*[6]

The interviewees also report that women are more likely to evaluate themselves on the basis of the erroneous assumption that competence requires individual, unaided achievement. This faulty conception often makes women reluctant to seek outside assistance for fear that others will interpret it as a sign of incompetence. Learning a job, however, necessitates asking questions. On a nationally televised panel of experts discussing the threat of nuclear war, Henry Kissinger unashamedly admitted that when he first became secretary of state he was stumped on how to handle a particular situation. He did not hem and haw about his incompetence—instead he drew on the experience of another by simply telephoning a former officeholder, Robert McNamara, to ask him what *he* would do. Kissinger knew that competence does not require one to know it all. Rather, one needs to know how to utilize the resources—people, information, money—that will enable one to carry out the job.

Why do so many women believe that competence requires them to be perfectly functioning, unassisted experts? One plausible explanation is that in the traditional female roles, as mothers and housewives, there are no straightforward standards of measurement or rewards for success. Housewives and mothers are not subjected to an end-of-the-year evaluation; they are not given or denied promotions on the basis of performance. This creates a dilemma for women as a group because "it's hard to give yourself a good grade on how well you are doing when it's not clear what 'good' really is."

A second reason that some women overestimate what it takes to be considered competent is their tendency to idealize people who occupy supposedly competent positions. They embellish these people with all kinds of mystical powers and abilities:

> It is not simply that women are obviously excluded from acquiring experience in the serious world of work . . . but that they actually come to believe that there is some special, inherent ability, some factor that escapes them and must inevitably escape them."[7]

Given women's inflated perception of competence, it stands to reason that they would come to share what has been called a "societal bias against the recognition of female competence."[8] As a result, women often fall prey to a kind of chronic self-doubt. Such women develop a great propensity for undervaluing or not recognizing their own skills, competencies, knowledge, and prior work and life experience. Instead, these women "assume incompetence," as vividly demonstrated by a career counselor at an Ivy League college:

> A young man will walk into my office who has a "C" average who will sit here confidently . . . expecting to get into law school and do well—which is fine, but at the same time I'll have a woman who is very bright, with a lot of credentials . . . a lot of experience, very intelligent who could definitely get into a good law school without any problem who will sit in panic and say, "I just don't think I will be good enough, I don't think I can get in."

In a sense, women's perceived need to be perfect may indeed be a rational response to the performance pressures placed on them by the larger culture. As one interviewee points out, "When you weigh the cost of it, a man can well afford to be less competent than a woman." The systematic discrimination women face necessitates that women try harder than men. Thus their sense of what is required to be judged competent may not be exaggerated at all but rather may be a realistic assessment of what women must do to achieve status in a male-dominated world. However realistic this assessment may be, perfectionism can and does interfere with women's ability to delegate effectively or otherwise carry out the mandates of their jobs.

Failure: It's Not What I Did, It's Me!

No one likes to fail. Yet failure and mistake-making are particularly troublesome for women. Women are more apt to overidentify with their failures, to assume more ownership for mistakes, to believe mistakes signal their ineptitude, to rebound less quickly from a setback, and to remember their errors longer. Said one career counselor:

> Women suffer more over their failures. They let them mean more that they need mean. Rather than realizing that there is life after

failure, they let their failures mean that they are inadequate or incompetent. They let their failures become proof to them that they aren't as qualified, rather than seeing a mistake or a failure as a human inevitability.

Failure, for a woman, can become so internalized that she identifies herself with the failure: "It is not the venture that failed, *I* am a failure." For women who identify too closely with their shortcomings, a critical evaluation of their performance can be devastating. "All of the positive feedback in the world can be wiped out by one criticism," notes a career counselor. "Criticism contributes to a woman's sense of incompetence," she adds, "causing tremendous suffering . . . because it is taken very personally: it's not what you did—it's *you*." Perhaps for this very reason, one management develoment specialist finds women to be "very clear on their failures, keeping memories of their failures long after their usefulness has died. I know women," she says, "who remember mistakes that they made in college jobs when they were working in the cafeteria!"

What compels women to store failures so clearly in their minds? For one, women have a general tendency to blame themselves when things go wrong.[9] Not surprisingly, failure and mistake-making are no exceptions. Even when external factors have worked against success, women will often take complete ownership of a disappointing endeavor. Many women seem willing to assume full responsibility for blunders that may rightfully belong elsewhere. They are often naive about the fact that errors may be the fault of other people, of organizational arrangements, or of deliberate attempts to sabotage their efforts.

The nagging feeling that "I should have done better" often stems from a sense many women share that they are simply not entitled to fail or to err. Beyond the fact that women generally feel undeserving, part of the reason relates back to women's own unrealistic definition of competence. If competence requires perfectionism, expertise, and unassisted achievement, then anything less is simply unacceptable.

Success: Luck, Charm, or Computer Error

Success, like failure, is problematic for women. In contrast to their overidentification with their failures, women are likely to *under-*

identify with their successes. For many, only grandiose accomplishments represent authentic successes. This may be attributed to some women's sense that success and achievement are exclusively male domains. Explained one career counselor:

> I don't think women identify with the word *achievement*. In fact, I give my clients a goal assessment worksheet which asks people to list their achievements, and women consistently balk at the word *achievement*. To them achievement means that you won the medal, or made it to the top, or it's just bigger than life. They can't identify themselves with what they see as a more male word.

Perhaps the most frequently used excuse for success is luck. Looking back, a university professor was convinced that she'd "lucked out" when she was accepted into graduate school, even when she was told she had submitted the best application the admissions panel had seen in two years. Similarly, in a recent *New York Times* interview, actress Mia Farrow revealed, "I always felt it was just some accident that they ended up using me instead of somebody else and with every movie I felt like I had to prove myself all over again."[10]

Closely aligned to the belief that success is a result of some fluke is the notion of being in the right place at the right time. One thirty-four-year-old accountant insists she was promoted from junior to senior accountant only because she just happened to have lunched with her boss on a day the boss "felt like promoting someone."

Still other ways women externalize their achievements is to credit them to factors such as the mistakes, goodwill, or efforts of others. One workshop participant still holds a nagging belief that her faculty review committee never actually read her master's thesis but instead put it on a scale and decided that at six pounds her research effort must have been substantial enough to merit a master's degree. Another example is the high school dropout who, after being deserted by her husband, returned to school, where she describes herself as having "jockeyed" a high school diploma. At age forty-two she passed her Scholastic Aptitude Test (SAT) examination and was accepted into college. She said she remembers thinking, "Oh, they like me, or they feel sorry for me because I'm older and they know I've got four kids." When she went on to make the dean's list, she assumed that "they wanted to balance the marking system so they put me on the upper end." This same woman is now herself a counselor at a private career development center for women. Hearing other women describe their accomplishments in terms of someone else's oversight, indifference, or pity has helped her to recognize her own self-negating tendencies.

A fourth way that women give away success is by attributing it to the assistance or collaboration of others. Such help presumably cancels out one's own contribution. Time and time again we hear women say, "if it weren't for my secretary," or, "if it weren't for my boss," or, "it was a team approach," or "the committee helped me." Observed one career counselor, "Somehow, some way, someone or everyone is responsible for our accomplishments except us!"

Still another way that women dismiss their accomplishments is by attributing them to the simplicity of the task. The types of disclaimers reported in interviews include such familiar one-liners as "anybody could've done it," "it was nothing," "if I did it, it can't mean much," and "it wasn't very hard." As one workshop participant summed it up, "I figure if *I* could get a Ph.D., anybody can." One interviewee insists that such comments are not indicative of false modesty but, rather, of the fact that women's achievements "frequently don't register very well."

Similarly, some women are afraid that if they are successful they will be expected to maintain the momentum of success or to repeat a commendable performance. According to one career counselor, the self-doubting woman may be held back by the belief that, "if I'm seen as being competent now they'll expect me to be competent down the road—and I know it's possible I won't be." "Even the most assured achievers are never entirely sure that they can repeat their triumphs," notes one writer, explaining, "the higher you fly, the more you worry about your staying power. . . ."[11]

Again, as with failure, women may be tentative about success because of the societal pressure they feel to perform competently. Interviewees talked about women's "fear of visibility . . . of being out there, of having to be on our toes." Success typically means being in a position where one's competency will be scrutinized even more closely, clearly a threat to those who fear being exposed as less than competent.

Perhaps for all these reasons, some women engage in behaviors designed to avoid or minimize the potential for future success or achievement. One strategy is simply to discontinue or reduce efforts following a successful accomplishment. One therapist observes that women cease to be able to perform as the stakes get higher. In the experience of a career counselor at a women's technical training school:

> They'll follow through on a difficult training program and because it was a real strain or struggle they'll say they need to rest to pamper themselves before looking for a job. So they take a week off, which is fine, but it becomes a month, and then it can lead to taking a temporary job at something lesser than what they were trained for.

When they doubt their capability to succeed, women frequently act in ways to curtail their own progress through self-sabotage. Even though the behavior is self-destructive, it is often preferable to the anxiety caused by success. A case in point is that of a "brilliant and intelligent woman" in the publishing field who, according to one training specialist, would "move right up to the point of success" and then, because she felt "unworthy," would "blow the moment of the challenge." Self-sabotage takes other forms—staying up too late the night before making an important presentation; substance abuse; or procrastination whereby one never quite finishes the novel, the thesis, the grant, or the painting.

Again, women have been described as suffering from an "atrophied sense of deserving." Thus it is conceivable that women may inhibit their own strivings for achievement out of a sense of not being entitled to expand or achieve occupationally. When a woman does not feel she deserves success, observed one career counselor, "the process of negotiating a change or moving upward can be a very painful process."

In summary, the yardsticks most women use to measure their own failures and successes are typically warped. Failures become internalized while achievements are externalized. Worse, women often do not believe they have the *right* either to fail or to succeeed. Thus, with respect to failure and success, women are left in a kind of achievement limbo. By overidentifying with one outcome, underidentifying with the other, feeling entitled to neither, and fearing both, they are denied an accurate internalized picture of their own abilities. Ultimately, this renders them unable to learn from their failures; to embrace their successes; and to exorcise the erroneous and crippling view of themselves as imposters, fakes, and frauds.

Unlearning Imposterism: The Road to Recovery

What can be done to break out of the constraining double bind of imposterism? It is our experience that this debilitating cycle can be stopped. Imposterism can be unlearned.

The method we use in our training workshops helps participants to identify, analyze, and then change their dysfunctional patterns. We focus on thoughts, feelings, and actions that reinforce imposterism and on changing these to support more positive and self-affirming behavior. This process is a tool that each woman can adapt to fit her own particular circumstances. We will illustrate each step in this process with examples from women who have attended our workshops. We invite you to fill in your own experiences for each step and see how this process works for you.

Step One: Focus on a Situation That
Triggers Your Imposter Feelings

First, get to know your pattern by focusing on a specific situation that triggers the feelings and behaviors of imposterism. Consciously begin to explore the details of the scene—the more concrete and vivid the better. Replaying a key scene in your mind like a home movie serves to illustrate your pattern in sharp detail.

Sarah, a corporate attorney and the only female in a large eastern firm, recalled her extreme anxiety the day she was presenting a case in court. Although she was well prepared and had a good case, she found herself obsessed with fears of mispronouncing a word—making some tiny slip that would prove her to be an incompetent fool. Despite her fears she performed successfully. When she returned to her apartment that evening, however, she was unable to acknowledge or enjoy her success. Instead, she felt a growing dread. She had been lucky, she said to herself. What would happen if she weren't so fortunate next time? To her own surprise, one day she found herself absentmindedly perusing the want ads for waitressing jobs. As she struggled to understand her own behavior, she realized that at least as a waitress she could be certain she knew what she was doing.

As Sarah related this story in one of our workshops, other women in the room nodded their heads knowingly. Though surprised that this clearly intelligent and capable woman should view herself as "inadequate, a fraud," they identified with the imposter feelings and behaviors her story so vividly illustrates.

Myra, a university professor, spoke of being unable to put pen to paper to carry out the publication requirements for her job. Despite high praise for her scholarship and research, she was certain she had passed her dissertation orals only because the committee members liked her. Each time she sat down to write, she froze up. As she sat at her desk, pen in hand, she imagined the ridicule her work would surely receive from other scholars should she ever dare to show it. She dutifully labored under this extreme self-criticism for hours, eventually quitting and tearing up whatever she had written in frustration and despair. After each writing session Myra began to imagine going back to teaching junior high school after the inevitable denial of tenure that loomed on the horizon.

These two accounts illustrate imposterism in that action. Despite clear evidence to the contrary, these talented and accomplished women persisted in feeling inadequate for the work they were trained to perform. By exposing these inner fears and self-doubts in all their painful detail, these women took the first step in unlearning imposterism.

Step Two: Take Stock of Your Thoughts,
Feelings, and Actions

An inventory of your thoughts, feelings, and actions in a particular situation begins to clarify the specific internal responses and complementary actions that form the core of the imposter syndrome for each particular woman.

Sarah, the attorney, made the following inventory of her experience in court:

Thoughts

I'm inarticulate.

I can't do this.

They'll see all my faults.

I know I'll say or do something really dumb.

I was lucky this time but can't do it again.

Feelings

Anxiety, fear

Frustration

Knot in stomach

Sweaty palms

Embarrassment

Depression

Actions

Spend an inordinate amount of time working on minor details.

Effective action taken but feels empty to me, a fluke.

Crying, overeating, perusing want ads for more suitable jobs (waitress, clerk, cashier, etc.).

In this case, the external manifestation and the internal experience are incongruent. Although Sarah is actually successful, she doesn't experience this success internally. Therefore, each time she appears before the court she again experiences herself as an imposter.

In Myra's case the internal experience and the outward actions are congruent and serve to prevent her from achieving success with writing. Her inventory:

Thoughts

I don't know enough.

I'm not smart enough.

This is too hard, which means I must be incapable.

Who do I think I am anyway?

Feelings

Anger at self

Frustration

Anxiety headache

Hopelessness

Actions

Spinning wheels, blanking out.

Agonizing over each word for hours.

Giving up and throwing away whatever I've managed to write.

Myra has a clear case of writer's block, a result of internal thoughts and feelings that reinforce her negative experience with writing and her continued failure to produce. A self-fulfilling prophecy is set in motion that prevents Myra from achieving her goals as a university professor and can ultimately lead to denial of tenure and loss of her position—a high price indeed.

Step Three: Name the Pattern Explicitly

The goal of the first three steps is to bring into clearer focus the vague feelings of uneasiness and personal inadequacy that are usually embedded in the imposter situation. We use a formula phrase that helps to pull together the data gathered in the first two steps and develop a concise pattern definition. Closer, more conscious examination is then possible, providing a framework for further exploration and the groundwork for eventual change.

Whenever I'm in a situation where _____.

I usually experience feelings of _____.

The negative voices in my head say _____.

What I typically do is _____.

In Sarah's case, the pattern clarification read as follows:

Whenever I'm in a situation where I'm presenting a case in court, I usually experience feelings of anxiety, fear, frustration, a knot in my stomach, sweaty palms. The negative voices in my head say: "I don't belong here, I can't do this. They'll discover all my faults, I know I'm going to blow it." What I typically do is spend an inordinate amount of time working on every little detail of the case, far longer and more exacting than anyone else would. I end up being successful but I don't feel good about it. Instead I feel lucky to have somehow slipped by them again. I say to myself, "Next time will I be so lucky?"

Step Four: Look at the Function

Although these patterns are in many ways self-defeating, they also serve a purpose. They were developed not because women are masochists, but because each of us is doing the best we can to protect ourselves under particular life circumstances. By identifying the function of imposter patterns, we can appreciate why we have maintained them. This information becomes helpful in developing strategies for change.

The following questions are helpful in identifying a pattern's protective function: What does this pattern help me get? What does it help me avoid? How does it protect or serve me?

At first, Myra insisted that there was no possible way her pattern helped. But when she persisted she discovered that her pattern of blocking whenever she sat down to write did indeed protect her. As long as she prevented herself from writing and showing her work to others, she avoided the risk of criticism and negative feedback. She could avoid making the inevitable mistakes and failures that accompany any new venture. She gained sympathy and support from friends and colleagues who commiserated with her. And she gained the safety involved in avoiding risk-taking.

Step Five: Finding the Crusher—Exposing the Lie

One core function all patterns serve is to protect us from what has been called the Crusher. The Crusher is a hidden, negative belief we hold about ourselves. At heart it is a basic feeling of inadequacy. The ultimate purpose of a pattern is to protect us from facing this negative core belief. The potential public exposure of the Crusher is so dreaded that the pattern becomes mild by comparison: "Better never to write anything down than to do so and confirm that I'm not capable."

One way to identify a Crusher is to imagine the statement you would most dread hearing someone say about you in the imposter situation. Sarah's worst fear while standing in court was to hear the phrase, "You'll never measure up." She could trace this Crusher to early experiences of always being compared to her older brother and feeling that no matter how hard she tried she would never be as smart, as personable, as successful as he. This was reinforced by messages from her father that it was inappropriate to aspire to be "like a man." Society contributed its share of strictures to support the Crusher for Sarah, as for many females in this culture.

Myra reflected on what her worst fear might be and instantly re-called herself in ninth grade, standing before class as her teacher ridiculed a project she had turned in. Her Crusher was, "I'm not capable of doing the difficult assignments," or simply, "I'm not capable." This experience capsulized her extreme fear of showing her work to others and her expectation of inevitable criticism and disapproval. Because she had been a bright, precocious child, she had received messages from her family that she should learn every-thing with ease, without struggle, with perfection. Thus when she encountered difficulty or received critical feedback, she saw it as evidence of her basic inadequacy rather than of the inevitable and normal failures that are a part of the learning process.

It is important to note that, even though they feel like the truth, *all Crushers are lies*! They are irrational beliefs about ourselves that simply are not true. A person may not have facility at certain tasks or may fail in particular attempts, but this is not justification for the categorical negative self-judgment that the Crusher represents. The fact remains, however, that too often these negative beliefs have been reinforced through interactions with family, friends, and teachers and further underscored by ideas in our culture about what women can and cannot do. Becuase we believe the Crusher to be true, we often act in ways that make it seem true, thus invoking a self-fulfilling prophecy.

Step Six: Assessing the Price of Your Pattern

Even though patterns serve a protective function, we pay a price. You never get something for nothing! Sarah realized that one price she paid for her pattern was that she never internalized the feeling of success and the sense of security for taking on risks and challenges such internal knowledge brings. She avoided taking on tough cases that would help her to grow and develop a reputation as an attorney. Her pattern precluded the excitement, challenge, and growth involved in flexing her legal mind and enjoying her own progress.

Similarly, Myra paid the price of never finding out what she could really do as a writer and scholar. Her pattern meant lost opportunities—not only to get the critical feedback that would help her develop confidence and facility as a writer, but also to receive recognition for her ideas. The ultimate price in her case would be to lose her faculty position, a victim of the publish-or-perish syndrome. Both women pay a financial price by holding themselves back.

Step Seven: Self-Support
Develop a Directional Statement

If you decide the price is too high, you are ready to design a plan of action for changing the pattern. A successful plan for change requires a foundation—a new attitude that will nourish and support new behaviors during the first uncomfortable stages of any process of change. This new attitude involves feeling entitled to be yourself, to make your own choices, and to express yourself freely in the world. All of us are entitled to these basic rights. But women too often don't believe in these basic entitlements.

Transforming the Crusher into a positive truth requires that we believe in our basic rights. This positive truth, which we call a *directional statement*, is the foundation of any positive change strategy.

Sarah designed the following directional statement for herself: "I measure up to myself and no one else. I deserve to appreciate my abilities and successes." Myra's directional statement was: "I'm capable of taking risks, learning from my mistakes, creating and sharing my ideas." She shortened this to "I am capable."

Ideally, the directional statement should be brief and punchy. It is also crucial to eliminate any hidden qualifiers: "I measure up to myself—but so what?" "I am capable—as long as people don't look too closely." It is important not to set up a demand for perfection: "I can measure up to the best lawyer of all time and never lose a case." "I am capable of doing anything brilliantly and with ease." Such expectations are neither realistic nor necessary for success. Imposing these demands on ourselves only fuels imposter feelings in the long run.

You will know your directional statement is on target if you can hardly bring yourself to think it, let alone say it out loud; if it engenders a physiological reaction such as blushing, sweaty palms, or a tight stomach; if it feels like a lie! Trust that you will overcome these reactions with practice and gradually begin to feel the rightness and truth of your statement. Just as athletes who mentally imagine successful performances *are* more successsful, so you can imagine yourself doing well and thereby increase the likelihood of effective change.

Step Eight: Brainstorming Alternatives

Supported by a firm belief in your basic rights and with a positive directional statement in hand, you are ready to design a plan of action. Begin by brainstorming all possibilities for new behaviors in the pattern situation. Go back to the original scene in step one and fantasize what you would really like to do instead. Brainstorm as many different possibilities as you can without censoring any of them. Sometimes the wildest ideas have just the kernel of creative possibility you need to implement a change.

Sarah brainstormed the following list of alternatives to help her begin to acknowledge her abilities as a lawyer. Next she rank-ordered these ideas, from most fearful to least fearful. Initially it is most effective to choose an action about which you feel relatively positive, beginning with the least fearsome options. Once one step has been taken, the next becomes easier, and we can begin to dispel the fears that prevent us from acting.

5—Ask for feedback from a lawyer I trust.

7—Find a mentor who is well established and well connected.

2—Write down every success I achieve and share it with a friend.

3—Make a list of new cases I want to try in the future, and work closely with others until I feel more confident.

1—Spend five minutes each morning imagining myself doing well in court, functioning with confidence and comfort.

4—Become more active in the women's bar association and help to mentor other women.

6—Talk to other female attorneys about their fears.

Step Nine: Make a Contract with Yourself

Make a contract with yourself that includes exactly what you plan to do, when, where, and by what date. This contract provides a clear framework that will support you when you feel overwhelmed, get stuck, or forget where you are heading. Sarah began networking more aggressively with other female attorneys with whom she could share her self-doubts and receive and give support. She began learning to give herself permission to mispronounce a word in court occasionally, yet still be a competent attorney.

Myra's contract with herself was to set aside two hours per week in which she would write freely without censoring or correcting her work. She arranged for a close friend to meet with her once a week to read her drafts, act as a sounding board, and provide critical feedback. She would use the feedback from these sessions to revise and rewrite. Once she developed a copy with which she was reasonably satisfied, she shared it with colleagues she trusted and respected. On the basis of their feedback, she made final revisions and then mailed the article to a journal. A second part of her plan was to interview five scholars she knew who were widely published and ask them for tips on how to work most effectively. They ended up being valuable contacts who provided direction on how to choose outlets and approach editors. As a result, Myra began to publish, to *feel* her success, to value criticism as a useful process, and ultimately to enjoy expressing herself through writing.

Both Sarah and Myra are well on the road to recovery. Each has a clear understanding of how her pattern works and has taken some concrete steps to intervene in the cycle. Like many other women, they have learned that imposterism can be stopped.

Other Strategies for Unlearning Imposterism

Women need to develop both personal and collective strategies for overcoming self-limiting doubts and philosophies so that they and society can benefit from all that fully functioning women have to offer. The few strategies we outline here are meant to be a jumping-off point. You are encouraged to create more.

Competence and Success

Avoid perfectionism. Don't hold yourself to impossibly high standards. Women need to realize that they need not persevere over every routine task, that some aspects of their job require only a mediocre performance. Not only is it all right to ask for help or to seek out others' opinions and feedback—it's downright competent to do so.

Consciously experiment with changing ritualistic behaviors and expectations. Instead of spending the night before an important work assignment preoccupied with everything that could go wrong, imagine doing well and feeling confident. Change the automatic "I can't" tape to "I can."

Set your sights on the next job. Recognize that although you may not yet possess all the information and skills needed to perform a given job, you are bright and resourceful enough to figure out how to acquire them once you get there.

Own your accomplishments, and catch yourself when you start to give them away. Your successes are not simply the result of good luck or harm. Personality certainly plays a role in some occupations, but it's only the icing on the cake—it's not the cake. Acknowledge the skills and effort that resulted in your success: "I got the account because I did my homework, planned my strategy carefully, and paid attention to my client's concerns." Not only does this positively reinforce your internal sense of accomplishment, but it also provides a good model for other women.

Keep a written record of your accomplishments. Observe how you dismiss, distort, or discount them. Learn to recognize when you are falling into the imposter trap, and refuse to do it.

Mentally recall all those you've "fooled." Imagine explaining how you tricked them into thinking you were competent, and imagine their reaction. A certain amount of arrogance is involved in maintaining the belief that your success is simply a result of fooling or charming someone else. Give those who recognize your abilities credit for knowing what they are doing.

Use the process described here to analyze your own experiences with self-limiting patterns. Design a directional statement you can use to affirm your entitlement to succeed and achieve. Post it on your mirror or over your desk, and repeat it often. Eventually you will internalize it and act on it automatically. Role-play acting out the opposite of your Crusher. Take on the character and actions of your positive imagination until it too becomes automatic.

Finally, as one observer puts it, fake it till you make it! You don't have to wait until you feel perfectly ready—that's another trap. Change your behaviors first, and the rest will follow. You'll be surprised how supportive others will be.

Individual and Collective Strategies

After examining your own pattern using the process just described, talk to other women. Share your experiences, doubts, fears, questions, and success strategies. Your silence, based on the mistaken assumption that "I'm the only one who feels this way," can lead others to collude in maintaining your fraudulent feelings. If we can talk openly about the fears, confusions, and misunderstandings that are a normal part of work, we demystify the roles that can lead to expectations for perfectionism.

As members of the work force, women need to introduce and support mentoring programs and network arrangements in their organizations that can support individual women, provide role models, share information and resources, and influence organizational policies and procedures. Together women can work to create a climate that values women and women's resources.

Up to now this discussion of the imposter syndrome, and our recommendations for interrupting it, have been largely focused on the individual. Yet organizations too pay a price when employees feel like imposters. Specifically, individuals who experience the imposter syndrome are:

Less likely to vie for advanced positions, creating an untapped labor pool.

More reticent about offering potentially valuable insights, solutions, ideas, and opinions for fear of being wrong or appearing stupid.

More apt to fall into the so-called expert trap by remaining in jobs in which they are comfortable and knowledgeable but which they have clearly outgrown.

Less likely to take risks from which the organization could gain.

Less able to internalize and thereby integrate praise and positive feedback.

Less able to make use of and grow from constructive criticism.

More likely to engage in costly procrastination.

More susceptible to psychological and physiological stress caused by the anxiety of waiting to be found out.

Therefore, organizations need to recognize and assess the following:

1. *What are the organizational norms relative to failure, risk-taking, mistake-making, and being wrong?* Does an employee have the right to be wrong occasionally, to have an off day, or to work at honing less-developed skills? Are employees encouraged to take risks? Are they pushed to learn from their mistakes or from failed risks? Are evaluations and supervision structured so as to reframe mistakes and/or weak areas as learning experiences? Are employees encouraged to engage in collaborative enterprises so that the consequences of risks are shared?

2. *What are the organizational norms relative to employees seeking assistance or information, or not knowing how to perform a task?* Is asking for help seen as a sign of weakness or as a legitimate request? Is admitting a gap in one's knowledge seen as normal and necessary for learning or as a sign of incompetence? Is perfectionism an unspoken rule?

3. *Are these organizational norms applied differently to women and men?* Are women unconsciously shielded from taking risks? Are

women given less challenging assignments? Are women allowed (with appropriate supports) to follow through on a tough assignment without being prematurely rescued? Are women given *more* challenging assignments as a test of their capabilities? Is mistake making—"getting egg on one's face—more acceptable for male employees? Is tooting one's own horn perceived differently when it is done by men than by women?

4. *Does the organization recognize and address the uniqueness of women's experience with respect to achievement?* Are appropriate steps taken to alleviate the problems of increased scrutiny and isolation that female advancement in the organization can bring? Since women have been found to lower their expectations for future success following a setback, is supervision based on a model of reframing, encouragement, and support? Given that self-doubt is most salient in new learning situations, particularly those where a woman is the first in a job area or position, is attention paid to providing appropriate training and support to women? Does the organization as a whole understand the kinds of external factors, both societal and organizational, that reinforce self-doubt in women: others' assumptions about women's abilities and appropriate female roles; women's outsider status in the work world; the different kinds and amount of feedback men and women receive from supervisors; the discounting behaviors of individual men in the organization; the pressures on women (as well as on members of minority groups, people with disabilities, and older workers) to represent to their entire social group; the pressures on women to prove their competence; the expectations that women excel in the multiple roles of worker, wife, and mother.

Given all these factors, training efforts in organizations need to focus on:

Providing a safe forum in which to express self-defeating fears and myths about competence, success, and failure.

Helping people learn to delegate—to let go of tasks they have insisted on carrying out personally because of their perfectionism.

Fostering risk-taking behavior.

Emphasizing the learning value of mistakes.

Building self-confidence.

Emphasizing that competence is typically a matter of acquired skills rather than a function of innate abilities.

Demystifying competence.

Recognizing self-negating language.

Helping people fully internalize or own their accomplishments so that they can proceed to build on them.

Examining the organizational norms as they relate to this topic.

Exploring the different ways these norms are experienced by women and men.

Exploring stereotypic assumptions about female ability, competence, and roles.

Assessing the behaviors of others that reinforce women's self-doubt.

Minimizing organizational pressures and recognizing social ones.

Making supervisors and mentors aware of the kinds of internal and external barriers undermining women's achievement potential.

Building support systems for women into the organizational structure.

Finally, both individuals and organizations must challenge ideas and policies that stereotype or categorize any group of people within the organization. Ideas and actions that undermine women and others on the basis of race, class, physical ability, age, and/or sexual orientation need to be challenged and changed so no one need feel she doesn't belong. We are all entitled to succeed, fail, test our competence, and grow. The more we affirm this for ourselves and others, the less potent imposter feelings become. The best antidote to imposterism may be authenticity—both individual and organizational.

Notes

1. P. Glance and S. Imes, "The Imposter Phenomenon in High Achieving Women: Dynamics and Therapeutic Interventions," *Psychotherapy: Therapy, Research and Practice 15*, (3).

2. J.C. Nichols, "Causal Attributions and other Achievement-Related Cognitions: Effects of Task Outcome, Attainment, Value, and Sex," *Journal of Personality and Social Psychology 31* (1975):379–389.

3. N.T. Feather, "Attribution of Responsibility and Valence of Success and Failure in Relation to Initial Confidence and Task Performance," *Journal of Abnormal and Social Psychology 13* (1969):129–144.

4. N. Chodorow, "Family Structure and Feminine Personality," in M. Rosaldo and L. Lamphere, eds., *Women, Culture, and Society* (Stanford, Calif.: Stanford University Press, 1974).

5. The experience of black women contrasts with this description. The recent spotlight on the ostensibly new problem of how to mix job and family has been met with bemusement by black women for whom, historically, "it wasn't something you *thought* about doing, you just did." "Our mothers instructed us that we were going to work, not marry and be sheltered," stated another black woman, adding, "it would be suicidal to believe we could do anything else."

6. B. Harragan, *Games Mother Never Taught You* (New York: Warner, 1977).

7. J. Miller, *Toward A New Psychology of Women* (Boston: Beacon Press, 1976).

8. V. O'Leary, "Some Attitudinal Barriers to Occupational Aspirations in Women," *Psychological Bulletin 81* (November 1978).

9. V.D. Crandall, W. Katkovsky, and V.J. Cranall, "Children's Beliefs in Their Own Control of Reinforcement in Intellectual-Academic Achievement Situations," *Child Development 36* (1965):91–109.

10. *The New York Times*, January 22, 1984.

11. C. Houck, "Triumphing Over the Fear of Success," *Cosmopolitan*, November 1982.

References

Barnett, R., and Baruch, G. 1978. *The Competent Woman.* New York: Irvington Publishers.

Baruch, G.; Barnett, R.; and Rivers, C. 1983. *Lifeprints.* New York: McGraw-Hill.

Crosby, F. 1982. *Relative Deprivation and Working Women.* Oxford University Press.

Kaufma, D., and Richardson, B. 1982. *Achievement and Women: Challenging the Assumptions.* New York: The Free Press.

LaBella, A., and Leach, D. 1983. *Personal Power.* Boulder, Colo.: New View Press.

Schenkel, S. 1984. *Giving Away Success.* New York: McGraw-Hill.

Weinstein, G. 1976. *Education of the Self: A Trainers Manual.* Amherst, Mass.: Mandala Press.

Young, V. 1985. "A Model of Internal Barriers to Women's Occupational Barriers." Ph.D. dissertation, University of Massachusetts.

4

Mentoring or Networking?
Strong and Weak Ties in
Career Development

Reba Keele

E very time I meet someone in top management I ask myself if
this person could be a mentor for me." A Harvard MBA, now
working as a manager in a large retailing chain, recently made this
comment to me. She reads the professional women's magazines
regularly and has had long discussions with her Harvard classmates
about career planning and development. She has heard it from all
sides: mentoring—forming a close relationship with someone higher
up in the organization who will take you under his or her wing and
show you the ropes—is essential if she wants to move up in the business world.

A similar trend is evident in today's business women's conferences, which usually include at least one display table arranged to
facilitate the exchange of business cards. Stacks of cards, in endless
rows, are carefully studied by the women before they select from
among them. Nor is this activity limited to the display tables: that
same conference will almost certainly include at least one workshop
on "networking"—building a list of contacts through business card
exchanges, phone calls, luncheons, and so on. Whereas the mentor
relationship is characteristically a close one, networking is more
casual. It is, however, no less crucial to one's success. Or so the experts and the popular business press would have us believe.

Career workshops, especially those designed for women and
minorities, place particular emphasis on mentoring and networking.

It should come as no surprise, then, that women feel pressured into developing such relationships. The realities of mentoring and networking, however, are more complex than the popular wisdom suggests. Both kinds of relationships should be examined more critically, for although both can be valuable in developing your career, each has limitations and even potential liabilities that must be recognized. Perhaps the best way to begin this examination is by looking at what we know about relationships—what sociologists call *social networks*—in general.

Strong and Weak Ties

A social network consists of all the people with whom I interact, ranging from close friends and family to people I call only when I have a particular need. Clearly, the ties or links I share with this broad range of people vary greatly in strength depending on the stability of the relationship; the extent to which I consider it binding; the demands it makes on my time, resources, and emotions; the confidences shared; and a host of other factors.

A useful analogy in conceptualizing the differences in strength of ties is that of a fishnet. Each knot is a person, and the strings between the knots are the ties between people. When you pull on my knot, those closest to me are most affected; the knots further away from me, though still connected to me, may not move at all. Those close and distant knots are, respectively, my strong ties and my weak ties.

Strong ties include kinship, friendship, and love relationships. Acquaintanceships and relationships based solely on their usefulness at particular times are considered weak ties. The most valuable weak ties are those that serve as bridges or connections between clusters of strong-tie relationships that would otherwise have no links. Strong ties tend to link people of similar backgrounds—people who usually move in the same social circles. My close friends and I tend to hear about the same things at the same time. Thus individuals with few weak ties are likely to get the same information that their good friends get. The only way to connect with new sources of information is through weak ties to distant parts of the fishnet. It is usually from my not-so-close friends, who move in different circles, that I receive news from other, more distant sources. That is why, for example, weak ties are often more useful than strong ties in providing information about job openings.

Weak ties also help maintain the structure of large networks (those with many people in them) that could not survive with strong ties alone. The reason is simple: nurturing strong ties requires so much time and effort that there is a self-limiting factor in the number of close relationships we can manage.

However valuable the weak ties in a network may be, one should not suppose that such contacts and acquaintances should therefore replace stronger ties. Your own experiences will tell you that greater support comes from strong ties, that people with strong ties are more motivated to assist each other and to be more available to each other. The important point here is that some types of assistance come more easily from strong ties than from weak ties, and some more easily from weak ties.

For example, imagine that your new boss seems to be a perfect candidate for serving as your mentor and that you are thinking of developing a closer relationship with him or her. Before taking any steps, however, you talk it over with one of your colleagues at your own level in the company. To your surprise, your colleague warns you away from getting closer to the boss, and points out all kinds of risks and dangers inherent in such a move. You wonder whether these warnings are altruistic or self-serving. Having a trusting and continuing relationship with the person giving the warning makes it easier to determine her motivation. In this case the strong tie is clearly valuable. On the other hand, a warning to avoid the company-sponsored aerobics classes in building 3, because that is a place where male employees ogle the female exercisers, requires no great attachment to evaluate.

Is the determining factor how personal the issue is, how much is at risk? Not necessarily. Strong-tie relationships may also have more "noise" attached to them. By *noise* I mean factors irrelevant to the issue at hand that nevertheless affect how both people respond. I was once told by a woman who was chosen along with me for participation in a special program that she could not work with me because my speech patterns "intimidated" her. Not wishing simply to dismiss the relationship, I pursued this further. Finally she said, "Well, maybe your patterns are like my mother's." That comment was certainly noise.

There are other kinds of noise as well. Noise might also be the reason that crucial feedback about performance that would be devastating from a mentor (a strong tie) might be acceptable from someone who works in another department. There is a far greater emotional investment in a mentor relationship, and comments intended as objective observations might easily be perceived as personal criticism. Other kinds of information, however, regardless of noise, might only be accepted from a strong-tie relationship. Ultimately, this is a matter of individual personalities and circumstances. For me, even positive information about characteristics that are virtually innate and would thus require great effort to change comes best from a friend who has some commitment to help.

Even in circumstances where both strong- and weak-tie relationships are available, one is often more effective than the other. Weak ties provide the greatest access to a variety of information, whereas coaching on the best way to deal with a difficult superior would likely be more trusted coming from someone known to be committed to your advancement. In a series of interviews with bankers conducted by one of my colleagues, it was commonly pointed out that outsiders—that is, weak-tie relationships—were consulted to assess the impact of innovations and new proposals. This checking was low cost in a way that discussing the proposal in house would not have been. Think of your own experiences in information trades: I most often learn information about my own department from strong ties, and information about people and actions in other departments or companies from weak ties.

The popular focus on mentoring, which is only one kind of strong tie, and on networking, which focuses only on weak ties, may actually do more harm than good. A social network focusing on both strong and weak ties will be responsive to a greater variety of career and personal needs.

Mentoring as a Strong Tie

A *Harvard Business Review* article entitled "Everybody Who Makes It Has a Mentor" demonstrates how extensively mentoring has been identified as an essential component of career development. Women especially have been counseled that the path to success and promotion is paved by the efforts of a mentor. Research indicates that people with mentors or sponsors earn more at a younger age, are more likely to follow a career plan, are more satisfied with their work, get more challenging job assignments, and gain a larger perspective of the organization and more visibility and job mobility. All these results are implicitly promised if one can only find a mentor. But what proportion of seekers are actually able to do so? Recent research suggests that the answer may be difficult to determine.

Frequency of Mentor Relationships

The frequency of mentoring is difficult to determine largely because the term is poorly defined. Two studies assert that mentoring relationships, though very important in careers, are more the exception than the rule.[1]

Another researcher received responses from 1,250 people who had announced new positions in the *Wall Street Journal*. He asked them, "At any stage of your career, have you had a relationship with a person who took a personal interest in your career and who guided or sponsored you?" More than 60 percent of the respondents answered "yes," claiming to have had, on the average, two such helpers.[2] Additional research claims that 65 percent of a sample of engineers and professionals reported having had a mentoring relationship.[3]

On the other hand, although my research found that an overwhelming majority of two samples (higher education and retailing) reported having helping relationships, no more than a third described these relationships as mentoring relationships. Instead, they were more often described as relationships with colleagues, friends, and bosses.

The reported frequency of mentoring varies both because researchers disagree on what the term *mentor* means and because at the moment it is socially desirable to have a mentor (even if you are not quite sure what one is). Is it right to place such emphasis on the mentor-protégé relationship? If only one-quarter of managers experience mentor-protégé relationships, as one of my studies found, then directives that demand the finding of a mentor do a disservice to those who invest a great deal of energy in trying to advance their careers in this manner. How can you tell whether you have a mentor or are likely to find one in your organization?

Definition of Mentor

What difference does it make whether *mentor* is used loosely or with some fidelity to the concept as it developed historically? The loose definition allows such assertions as this one from a book directed at managerial women: "If women want to succeed, they need to be mentored into these positions traditionally held by men"; or that the only times women don't need mentors are when they are "content" and when there are no real opportunities for movement.[4] Such prescriptions, when read by women in preparation for management careers or at the entry level, may lead to wasted time and energy.

Some writers have defined a *mentor* as anyone who takes a personal interest in your career and who guides or sponsors you, or as a person who significantly helps you reach your major life goals. This definition even includes professional career counselors whom you pay for their services. Clearly, people who fit those definitions are useful in career development, but they are not mentors. A mentor relationship is one in which the person higher in the organization or more experienced serves as coach, teacher, exemplar, counselor, provider of moral support, and facilitator of the realization of the protégé's dream.[5] The relationship has the intensity of that between parent and child, or between siblings, and lasts from two to ten years. A mentor relationship is an example of a very strong tie.

Clearly, those who define *mentor* more restrictively find fewer such relationships than do those who define the term very broadly. The problem seems to be that different researchers are talking about a variety of strong-tie relationships and calling them all *mentor-protégé*. But only a quarter of us will have the opportunity of having a true mentor. Instead, most of us will have a variety of strong-tie relationships that do not have the closeness and intensity of mentoring but that are useful to our careers. In my research, interviewees have identified spouses, landladies, friends, faculty only three or four years ahead of them, and people they have met on committees of national organizations as having had significant impact on their advancement. None of these people were mentors.

Is it useful, then, to expend a great deal of energy, as the Harvard MBA at the beginning of this chapter did, in searching for a mentor? Is it not more efficient to identify the people we depend on for accomplishing what we need to do and then to establish the kind of tie with them that makes sense and is available to us?

Availability of Strong-Tie Relationships

Researchers at last have documented what every professional woman already knew: that highly educated white males in formal positions of authority are more likely to be central in the organization's networks. (Or, in other words, the knots of white managers are most likely to be in the center of the fishnet, with lines out in all directions.) This central position makes it more likely that those white males will have the most ties of both sorts. One study develops a strong case for the fact that organizational members seek other persons like themselves because likeness decreases organizational uncertainty and strengthens communication.[6] Women and minorities will find it more difficult to form strong ties, especially with the white males who are most centrally located, because of their dissimilarity to these individuals and their distance from the center of the fishnet.

Support for the truth of that statement came from interviews with male mentors of female protégés. The study pointed out that the males waited to establish relationships with the women until the protégés had established themselves because of the visibility of the women and the difficulties of cross-sex relationships.[7] Women may be selected as protégés for different reasons than men—for instance, to show a company's commitment to affirmative action, or to prove that a male mentor can take on what is seen as a difficult management problem. Regardless of the circumstances, then, one can see that establishing a mentor relationship is not likely to be an easy task for a woman.

Networking as Weak Ties

A second theme in the popular literature is *networking*, which emphasizes the exchange of general information and professional support. One company I know about has supported the development of black work groups and women's work groups to provide sources of information and support for its members. Many formally organized networks for women (such as Zonta) are similar to Kiwanis or Rotary. In Salt Lake City a few years ago, twenty or so women established a formal network called the Women's Information Network (WIN). When I first spoke to them, five or six years ago, they were fifteen women who met each month above one member's retail establishment. Two months ago I spoke to a group of seventy-five WIN members at one of four different chapters meeting each month. They meet to gather new information that is helpful professionally, to exchange job information, and to meet people who might be useful to them in some way later on.

Members of WIN and other similar networks exchange business cards and lunch invitations or use other methods to increase business exposure and information. The emphasis is on weak ties. In the words of one student of the field:

> These new people you're going to meet . . . will be added to your network for strictly business reasons. . . . You don't have to like the people you network with. . . . So try to set your personal and political life to one side as you build your work-related network. Include people for their jobs, their expertise, and their connections, not for their personal attractiveness or its lack.[8]

In contrast to mentoring advocates, who ignore weak ties, networkers focus on the role of weak ties. Both types of relationships have been proposed separately as the answer to career development problems. But a focus on either is too narrow. Only by learning from research on social networks can we understand the roles of different kinds of relationships in career development and avoid a simplistic focus on mentoring and networking.

Social Networks as Strong- and Weak-Tie Relationships

To understand what kinds of relationships are most important for career development, we need to consider the pressures on people toward strong or weak ties and the impact of the person's sense of security on their choice of ties. Strong and weak ties exist in both friendship and organizational networks. Understanding their complexity will help clarify the kinds of relationships helpful to individual careers.

Pressures toward Strong and Weak Ties

What counsel would I give to someone just entering a job (low-status) or to women at middle-management levels (typically with less power than men) about the kinds of relationships they should build? It will likely be ineffective, over the long term, to focus on mentoring or networking, largely because of women's lack of status or power.

The advantage of using weak ties to obtain jobs is greatest for those with the lowest status; the advantage diminishes as status increases. Think of it this way: as I become more powerful in the organization and have higher status, I gain access to peers (who are probably strong ties) who have more information than was true when my peers were low-status. If I am a middle manager, my sources of information about jobs in other companies will probably come from a friend of a friend. If I am the chief executive officer (CEO), my information about a new job will be more likely to come from a peer.

Focusing on mentoring alone can make weak ties less effective and less available. A female researcher interviewed 10 of the 100 top female executives in the country who reported mentoring relationships. Eight of them reported feelings of isolation, both in the workplace and from social activities of work colleagues. "For the women in this study there were no real peers, either among the women or among the men. There was only the mentor."[9] As I pointed out earlier, much energy and time is required to nurture strong-tie relationships. Thus one reason for the isolation these women feel has to be that, in focusing on the mentor/protégé relationship, they are walling themselves off from other, perhaps equally valuable and productive relationships.

Low-status, low-power people who wish to succeed will look for ways to increase both status and power. The less I have to trade to another person in exchange for their help or support, the more vulnerable I am to the person who controls the resources or information that I need. Theorists suggest that one way to balance power is to extend the number of people we relate to, creating new tradeoffs and greater access to resources by adding new members to the network.

An example of this process occurred for me when I was appointed to the Board of Regents for public higher education in my state. I was not the first woman appointed, but I was the first woman with a higher-education background, and was clearly low-status (female) and low-power (newly appointed). There were so many undercurrents and so much power brokering going on that I knew I would remain low-status and low-power unless I had something to trade.

There were several ways that I gained status and power through building a network (fishnet) of relevant people. I met press people and asked them for information, selected two or three knowledgeable men from whom I sought counsel, and strengthened my contacts with women on various campuses who could give me useful information about proposals or people. I traded information for information and tried to become the most knowledgeable person on curriculum matters. Within a year I was chairing the Curriculum and Roles committee and was elected to the Executive Committee. I still have less power than the prominent businessmen who enjoy special credibility because of their financial expertise, but I am now in a position to bring about change on issues that matter to me.

This kind of network expansion is impossible in exclusive mentoring relationships because of the time investment such relationships require. Those women who were isolated remained with the mentor: they did not seek out other sources from which to obtain the benefits the mentor provided. If, feeling a lack of power, I choose to extend my network as a way of obtaining more power, then the pressure in the system will be toward weaker ties. Such a strategy requires less energy—and time—to nurture and sustain than would a strategy that involved creating new strong ties.

A second method of balancing power is to consolidate networks or to create coalitions of different networks. Coalitions naturally tend to create stronger ties through increasing interaction among people in the coalition. The size of the network will, however, play an important part in characterizing the relationships. In one state an organization called the Consortium for Women in Higher Education is an effective coalition for women seeking promotions and research opportunities. They keep each other informed of positions available and of tactics that work effectively in the political process of tenure. The group has provided connections for co-authoring. The members are able, as a coalition, to make it less likely that only the men in their departments have access to information about, for example, salaries and position openings. Initially the group also formed close friendships. As more women have joined and membership has changed, however, the relationships have changed to include more weak ties.

Group size affects the strength of ties. The complexity of relationships in a network increases at a faster rate than the size of the organization, and the larger the number of ties, the more the strength of the ties diminishes. The more people an individual must depend on to accomplish her work, the more ties will be required. Strong ties require sustained interaction time; as the size of the group increases, less time is available for each interaction. This may partially explain the isolation experienced by the protégés mentioned earlier: The mentoring relationship absorbed so much time that, albeit unintentionally, all other relationships suffered.

Effect of Insecurity

Although it is difficult for women and minorities in organizations to develop the kinds of strong-tie relationships they need to increase their power, they will still feel pressure to establish such ties as a way of lessening their relative insecurity. The more vulnerable an individual is to strong consequences from events beyond her control, the more insecure she is in her organization. (For instance, the assembler of computer chips faces layoff as a result of changes in defense policy or economic conditions in the rest of the industry.) The more insecure she is in her organization, the more pressure there will be for her to depend strongly on one or more individuals who can offer protection from those events. The more resources I have (whether they be money, information, supportive individuals, education, or whatever), the more I can resist becoming dependent on a few individuals.

From this argument, the person most likely to depend on strong ties would be the person with the fewest resources (economic, emotional, intellectual) or skills. Ironically, since strong ties depend more on a mutual ability to respond to needs than do weak ties, the person with fewer weak ties is likely to have less to offer to a strong-tie relationship than does the person with other resources. My colleague Mary DeLaMare-Schaefer and I refer to this as the *credit theory* of mentoring: to get credit, one must demonstrate that it is not really needed; those most likely to be attractive as protégés for a mentor are those who demonstrate that other people, skills, and contacts are available to them. Especially in career relationships, it appears, "them that has gets."

Evidence for Social Networks in Career Development

Although there are some studies that examine social networks in organizations, little has been done to examine the role in career development of a network composed of both strong and weak ties. The focus has been primarily on mentoring and secondarily on networking. The social network, however, composed of strong and weak ties of varying types and intensities (possibly including a mentor), has many advantages over the highly touted mentor-protégé relationship. A focus on finding a mentor may prevent a woman from building the variety of relationships that will lessen her dependence and increase her value to her organization. When that happens, she *increases* her insecurity in the organization and *decreases* her chances of finding a mentor. In short, the focus on mentoring actually decreases the chance that mentoring will occur.

To make that point more clearly, some comparisons between a mentor-protégé relationship and a social network are useful. A mentor-protégé relationship is relatively exclusive, ranging from one to probably no more than three or four protégés. In contrast, a social network may include hundreds of people.

Mentor relationships are, moreover, typically limited to those in higher positions in the organization, whereas a social network includes ties with superiors, subordinates, subordinates of peers, peers, suppliers, bankers, and anyone else who can provide the person with needed resources. In John Kotter's study of general managers, he describes a manager whose subordinates reported that he knew a thousand people by name.[10] Most networks include many more people than might be assumed—often hundreds.

Mentoring relationships may last for some time but are inherently time-limited, in part because of the intensity of the relationship. Within a social network there will be relationships of varying durations, depending on the strength of ties, the amount of reciprocity, and the needs of the central person.

The mentor relationship involves a high level of investment for both parties; it is a strong tie nearly equal to a family connection. That very intensity may affect the availability of the relationship to women and minorities. As we have seen, most people in a position to be mentors are white males. In less intense relationships, racial and sexual differences are less important because the two people are not strongly linked together. When a protégé is closely linked in others' minds with a mentor, however, those same racial and sexual differences assume a new importance. Gossip may not start if I work with a *number* of males, but spending a lot of work time or being intensely involved with one particular male will almost certainly trigger some gossip. Most mentors don't want that excess baggage in addition to the not inconsiderable burden of being a mentor.

It is in the nature of mentor relationships that the focus is on the mentor's agenda; the greatest reciprocity in the relationship arises from the fact that the protégé can advance the mentor's goals by doing the kind of legwork that makes the mentor look good. By contrast, I structure my network so that it accomplishes my own agenda. The reciprocity I offer to others may be information, or praise, or a good word to their boss; by its nature it is less restrictive.

The mentor has more power in establishing the relationship than does the protégé. One does not just say, "Hi, will you be my mentor?" (although some women have tried). Although the feelings must be mutual, the mentor controls whether the relationship is ever established. Again, in the social network I have much control over membership because I am not asking for the same kind of intense support and help.

The protégé is dependent on the resources of the mentor. The mentor is typically the primary provider of emotional, appraisal, informational, and instrumental support for the protégé.[11] The social network can provide the same kinds of support, but because it will come from many relationships rather than one or two, that support is more likely to be found.

The most descriptive study of the impact of a social network on career development is that reported by Kotter. He studied general managers, examined their appointment books and other papers, and talked to those who worked with them. The managers successfully built networks adequate to the tasks or agendas they had set for themselves. The networks were very large, included strong and weak ties (including some mentor-protégé relationships), and were composed of those people on whom the managers depended to accomplish their goals. Kotter judged to be least effective in their positions those who were least effective at building a network of mutual obligation.

Our own research supports Kotter's observations. A colleague and I asked bankers to talk about their networks and represent them visually. On average, each person drew three concentric circles. The further out the circles, the weaker the tie. The pattern that emerged was quite interesting: again on average, each circle contained roughly twice as many people as the circle preceding it. Fifty-nine percent of those contacts are inside the organization, 41 percent outside—another indicator of different kinds of contact. This supports other findings about large networks and the assumption that meaningful contacts include both strong and weak ties. When interviewed, our bankers reported that the concentric circles describe a small core group to whom they go for many different kinds of support, surrounded by a larger group of people whose function might be quite specialized; 42 percent of the support they receive is informational. None of the 100 respondents reported having only a core group. Our findings, together with those reported by Kotter and others, strongly attest to the importance for career development and productivity of a network that contains both strong and weak ties as sources of the four kinds of support mentioned earlier.

Summary

The vast amount of material that has been published on mentoring does not seem consistent until one understands that different studies talk about relationships of different degrees of strength. When career development literature is placed in the context of social-network research, both strong and weak ties are seen to be important.

Seen in these terms, it becomes clear that too strong a focus on one kind of relationship leads to neglect of the importance of the other.

Research indicates that strong-tie relationships may not be equally available to all members of a network, and that women and minorities, who probably have less stability and power in the organization, may need to focus on weak ties to balance the lack of availability of strong ties. Network expansion is one way to overcome power imbalances; but the larger a network becomes, the weaker the ties become, so there is probably an upper limit to the number of ties that can be formed.

Because women are relatively more insecure in their positions and of lower status in organizations, they may be more dependent on strong-tie relationships. Ironically, as we have seen, those with large weak-tie networks are more likely to be able to build strong-tie relationships because they have more to offer to those connected with them.

Women and members of minority groups have not advanced as rapidly as they would like. But the dilemma of career advancement for women and nonwhite minorities cannot be solved by simplistic prescriptions. Both mentoring and networking are often presented as separate solutions that will bring about equity in organizations. By focusing exclusively on either mentoring or networking, however, individuals of either sex or any race are likely to hinder their access to the information and resources available in their organization.

What, then, should individual women do, either as employees or as managers? What should organizations do? Organizations need to abandon assigned mentoring programs, which are typically ineffective and sometimes create a sense of betrayed expectations. Instead, they need to provide opportunities for employees from different areas to meet each other. That can be done at many levels— interdepartmental task forces, socials, transfers among departments. They need to support employees attending the kinds of workshops and training sessions that will put them in contact with others from their industry. The fact that the organization values cross-departmental and cross-level contact needs to be communicated verbally and symbolically.

Finally, individuals need to identify all the people on whom they depend to accomplish their own agenda, and set about connecting with those people. It is not necessary to be someone's best friend to have something useful to trade. Consciously build a large, diverse fishnet and spend your energy on many different kinds of connections, without desperately seeking a mentor or pointlessly collecting business cards.

Notes

1. E.G.C. Collins and P. Scott, "Everyone Who Makes It Has a Mentor," *Harvard Business Review* 56 (1978):89–101; D.J. Levinson, C.N. Darrow, E.B. Klein, M.H. Levinson, and B. McKee, *The Seasons of a Man's Life* (New York: Knopf, 1978); R.M. Kanter, *Men and Women of the Corporation* (New York: Basic Books, 1977).
2. G.R. Roche, "Much Ado about Mentors," *Harvard Business Review* 57 (1979):14–20, 24–28.
3. G.W. Dalton and P.H. Thompson, *Novations: Strategies for Career Management* (Glenview, Ill.: Scott, Foresman, 1986).
4. N.W. Collins, *Professional Women and their Mentors* (Englewood Cliffs, N.J.: Prentice-Hall, 1983).
5. Levinson et al., *Seasons*.
6. Kanter, *Men and Women*.
7. L.W. Fitt and D.A. Newton, "When the Mentor is a Man and the Protégé is a Woman," *Harvard Business Review* 59 (March–April 1981):55–60.
8. M.S. Welch, *Networking: The Great New Way for Women to Get Ahead* (New York: Warner Books, 1980), pp. 87–88.
9. A.K. Missirian, *The Corporate Connection: Why Executive Women Need Mentors to Reach the Top* (Englewood Cliffs, N.J.: Prentice-Hall 1982), p. 60.
10. J.P. Kotter, *The General Managers* (New York: The Free Press, 1982).
11. J.S. House, *Work Stress and Social Support* (Menlo Park, Calif.: Addison-Wesley, 1981).

5

Sexual Attraction at Work: Managing the Heart

Duncan Spelman
Marcy Crary
Kathy E. Kram
James G. Clawson

Male–female attraction in the workplace—the subject seems to hit a sensitive nerve in almost everyone. Think how quickly the national media picked up on the story of Mary Cunningham and William Agee at Bendix. Front-page articles appeared day after day in virtually all the major newspapers, bringing Cunningham and Agee instant fame—some would say notoriety—and elevated the story of their affair to near-mythic status. Across the country, countless people might not be able to say what the Bendix Corporation does—but chances are they'll know Mary Cunningham's name.

Similarly, an article by Eliza Collins entitled "Managers and Lovers," published in the *Harvard Business Review*, prompted a number of emotional letters—some signed, some anonymous—from readers who for one reason or another were upset by her discussion of love relationships in the office. Moving romance from somewhere out there into the workplace dramatically changes the way people think. Love, we are told, is blind—but not in the office. Everyone loves a lover—but not in the office.

You will probably not find yourself or your relationships the center of attention that Mary Cunningham and her relationship with William Agee were. Yet the special feelings you may have for a co-worker of the opposite sex could complicate your professional and private life just as significantly as it did Cunningham's. Sometimes you will be able to manage such feelings easily; they will be only a pleasant addition to life on the job. But probably not always. For example, put yourself in Sue Bredbeck's place in the following situation.

The Case of Sue Bredbeck and Doug O'Connor

Sue had been employed at the Prospect Company for eighteen months when she met Doug O'Connor at a friend's party. Doug also worked for Prospect, as the team leader of a new product development team. The two of them hit it off immediately, dividing their conversation between talk about work and discussion of common interests in skiing, science fiction, and alumni activities at the local university of which they both were graduates.

Over the next couple of months the relationship between Sue and Doug developed, although it was not romantic. They went to lunch together fairly regularly, joined mutual friends for ski weekends, and attended basketball games at their alma mater, but never really had a serious date.

After Sue had known Doug for about six months, she raised the possibility of joining his project team. She was working in a much less exciting part of the company and had been looking for an opportunity to become involved in a position that would be more interesting and would allow her to showcase her abilities. After lengthy discussions of Sue's background and career goals, the team's work, and Doug's needs, Sue and Doug agreed it would make sense for both Sue and the team if she joined Doug's group.

Sue's initial experiences with the team were both exciting and confounding. The work itself was very stimulating, but she was disturbed about the cool reception she received from the men and women on the team. Doug had described them as an extremely close-knit group that enjoyed an easygoing, friendly, productive approach to their work—and drinks together after work on a fairly regular basis. But Sue's experience with the team members seemed quite formal to her, and she was not invited to any after-work social gatherings.

Doug, too, was concerned. During one of their frequent lunches together he mentioned to Sue that he had noticed a tension in team meetings that had not existed before. The familiar banter was absent, and communications seemed to be flowing less freely.

Once they had voiced their shared concerns, Sue and Doug spent many hours trying to diagnose the sources of the problem. Following one such conversation over dinner after work on a Friday, the discussion became more personal and ended with both Sue and Doug expressing a desire for their relationship to become "more than friendship." They agreed to go away for a romantic weekend together.

Over the next few weeks life on the project team became both better and worse for Sue and Doug. After a brief period in which they had some difficulty concentrating on their work because of the intensity of their new relationship, they soon found themselves working together extremely well. Their joint efforts were exciting and very productive. But the other members of the team were increasingly cool toward Doug and cold toward Sue. The once smoothly functioning team was in trouble.

One day Doug's boss pulled him aside and told him he had heard through the grapevine about problems in the project team because of a romance. He told Doug to identify the people involved and put a stop to it before things got out of hand. Now Doug was unsure how to handle the situation. The effectiveness of his team had been disrupted, and his boss was unhappy about a mystery romance of which Doug himself was a part. Yet Doug's relationship with Sue was a source of both personal and professional satisfaction.

Sue, concerned about her relationships with her co-workers, decided to pay a visit to Karen Boyer in the Human Resources Department. During her orientation to the company, Sue had been particularly impressed with Karen's presentation on the unique challenges faced by women at Prospect. Karen suggested to Sue that the team members might feel threatened by her relationship with Doug, even if there was no real reason for them to worry. Karen also asked Sue if she had considered fully the potential consequences of the relationship. Sue left with misgivings about her decision to become involved with Doug. She focused especially on what would happen if the relationship soured. She also worried about whether people would assume she was trying to "sleep her way to the top."

Sue Bredbeck is confronted with the challenge of managing male-female attraction at work (as is Doug O'Connor, of course). She feels caught between her own positive feelings about the relationship and the negative reactions of outsiders. She had not anticipated such negative reactions, nor does she understand them. In addition, she is beginning to be aware of some personal dangers in the relationship.

Finding yourself attracted to someone you work with is much more complicated than an attraction to someone outside work. Your personal and professional life are intensely joined. Attraction outside work undoubtedly affects your professional life (and vice versa)—but only indirectly. When the attraction occurs within the organization, however, the effects are likely to be more direct and powerful. If an intimate relationship develops, you are putting many of your eggs in a single basket. Working relationships can be greatly strengthened when co-workers are drawn to each other and new lines of communication are opened. Work can become a setting for deep personal as well as professional satisfaction. Should the relationship turn sour, however, it can damage two key spheres of your life, and it can be very difficult indeed to get away from the pain.

Attraction has doubtless always been present in the workplace. But the movement of women into functions that were previously all male increases the opportunities for such attraction to occur and also increases the weight of the potential consequences, whether positive or negative. What's more, the greater numbers of women in the work force, together with an elevated divorce rate and changing patterns in marriage and employment, result in the presence of more single people on the job, making the office a far more important social setting.

Women (and men) now face new issues. As a woman, you are an unfamiliar newcomer and a member of a minority group at work. Attention is focused on everything you do. Your response to the complexities of these attractions can affect your day-to-day satisfaction and productivity at work, your career progress, and the effectiveness of the organizations for which you work.

How Attraction Happens

The problems we are talking about here go beyond sexual attraction. Women and men can be drawn to each other and a relationship can become quite intimate without sexual stirrings occurring.

People hold different attitudes about the relationship between intimacy and a sexual relationship. Some necessarily link the two—one being necessary for the other and vice versa—and others see them as separate. Accordingly, in discussing a relationship that is intimate, we will not assume that the relationship includes a sexual component.

Still, we can't ignore the fact that as attraction develops between women and men who work together, one of the ways in which the two people may be attracted to each other is sexual. As women and men struggle with the attraction they feel for each other and what to do about it, the question of whether the relationship will be sexual is often central in their minds. It is important, therefore, to determine the roles of sexual attraction and sexual dynamics.

It is interesting—and certainly important—to note that the individuals involved in a relationship generally seem more able to entertain the possibility of an intimate relationship that is nonsexual than are the outsiders observing it. Indeed, people who observe attraction occurring between two co-workers often assume a sexual relationship exists before it really does, or, at least, are deeply interested in whether such a relationship develops. This tendency appears to operate at a primal level. Basic, deeply emotional issues seem to be involved. We probably all react more strongly and less rationally to sexual issues than to almost anything else. If these issues are played out in the workplace, the situation becomes even more problematic.

The Consequences of Attraction

In seeking to manage attraction at work, you need to keep in mind what's at stake. There are potential consequences—both positive and negative—that a relationship can have for you, your career, your co-workers, and even your organization.

The positive consequences that can result when two co-workers are drawn together often receive far less attention than the negative ones. In addition to whatever personal gratification you might experience in the relationship, interpersonal attraction can be good for you professionally and good for the organization. Clearly, your career will not develop—at least not to its fullest potential—if you interact with others solely through formal roles. Informal relationships—friendships—open us up to less constrained forms of communication and provide us with a wide range of valuable resources: ideas, expertise, time, money, information, and an expanding network of personal contacts.

Similarly, organizations can enjoy increased productivity and creativity from people who develop relationships that permit them to interact with co-workers as total human beings rather than only in their work roles. Attraction can be the basis for more interesting, supportive, and developmental relationships. And there is clear benefit to the company as the relationship shifts from superior/subordinate to mentor/protégé, from mere co-worker to colleague.

But it is equally true that you may face negative consequences if you are attracted to someone you work with (in fact, these consequences may surface if your co-workers *believe* you to be attracted, or even if you are the object of someone else's attention). Your career may suffer if your attention to work is reduced (or believed to be) by your involvement with a co-worker. Likewise, if your professional judgment is compromised (or believed to be) by interpersonal dynamics, your position may be damaged. And as Sue and Doug's experience shows, your co-workers may well feel threatened by your relationship, and you could face not support and warmth but anger, jealousy, or resentment.

Moreover, work may become quite stressful if you find yourself in a situation where the attraction is not mutual. This situation can be particularly difficult if the other party has significant control over your future in the organization.

Unfortunately, it seems that managers are more likely to cause negative consequences than positive ones when their subordinates are confronted with handling attraction. The reaction of Doug's boss is not terribly unusual. Managers frequently feel overwhelmed or uncomfortable and, as a result, either avoid the matter entirely or overreact.

Overall, negative consequences are probably more likely than positive ones. And, unfortunately, because women have less seniority than men in most organizations, they will probably continue to bear the brunt of the negative consequences. Few of us have been prepared to deal effectively with the complex emotions evoked by attraction at work. Indeed, until we are involved in such a relationship ourselves, we are apt to view our jobs and our love lives as occupying two separate worlds. Still, much as we might prefer to prevent attraction from occurring, to keep these worlds separate, such relationships *will* develop. We need, instead, to increase our understanding so we can benefit from the positive consequences and minimize the negative. In short, we need, as far as possible, to manage these relationships rather than having them manage us.

Understanding Attraction at Work

A full range of forces come into play when you are attracted to a co-worker. These forces must be understood and managed if you hope to respond effectively. Approaches that fail to deal with them will be unsuccessful at best and harmful at worst. Some means must be found to sort rationally through the complexity in order to avoid being immobilized. The forces relevant to attraction can be sorted into four different groups, beginning with those within you and moving progressively outward:

1. Within you.
2. In the interaction between you and the other person.
3. In the work group(s) of which the two of you are a part.
4. In the organization for which you work.

Each of these forces will influence whether or not attraction develops, what consequences it will have if it does, and how it can best be managed by you and others in your organization.

These forces, personal as well as organizational, exist in the larger setting of a social culture. Specifically, the beliefs and mores of the community in which your organization is located can influence organizational policies and practices, the attitudes and reactions of co-workers, and the way people generally interact in the workplace. For example, a woman and man working together in an organization in a small midwestern town would probably face more sanctions against becoming attracted to each other than would a similar pair of individuals working in Los Angeles or New York. Similarly, societal trends regarding relationships between men and women and the "appropriate" roles for each sex also affect attraction at work. Both men and women are now regularly employed in jobs that twenty-five years ago would have been seen as bizarre for someone of their sex. There is, moreover, a greater tolerance for premarital and extramarital sexual relations now than there was twenty years ago. As such trends continue to evolve, they may well have further impact on whether attraction will develop, what effect it will have, and how it can be managed.

Forces within You

Each of us brings a unique history of attitudes, abilities, and experiences to our workplace relationships. We have differing abilities to let others in or keep them out, different ways of approaching each other. Broadly speaking, three personal factors are significant with relation to male-female attraction: (1) your attitudes, values, and beliefs regarding such relationships, especially at work; (2) the personal needs that are expressed in the relationship; and (3) interpersonal competence.

Attitudes, Values, and Beliefs

Your ideas about the rightness or wrongness of various kinds of relationships with co-workers, as well as your beliefs about how such relationships affect career progress, will influence whether and how you become involved, what impact involvement will have on you and others, and how you will manage the situation.

All of us received messages in our early lives about relationships with people of the other sex. Your core attitudes about how close or distant to be with co-workers began to be formed in childhood. Of course, these central beliefs may have been modified by your experiences at work and elsewhere. Good or bad experiences—both your own and those you've observed—have led you to develop rules of thumb about how close to get to co-workers.

Sue and Doug seemed comfortable with becoming involved in a friendship and ultimately a romance with a co-worker. Other people are much less willing to become involved with co-workers beyond their work roles; they believe such involvement to be dangerous. Still others cultivate personal relationships for the express purpose of furthering their career progress and accomplishing the work at hand.

You can probably reduce the likelihood of becoming involved in a relationship you don't want, or in a way you don't want, by clarifying your values and checking your assumptions. Sue and Doug, for example, seemed to be unaware of the potential costs of her joining Doug's team and of their becoming romantically involved. Had they examined their beliefs about such relationships, they might have anticipated the personal and professional problems they eventually ran into. On the other hand, individuals may also discover that their attitudes, values, or beliefs are needlessly causing them to close themselves off from new and more intimate relationships. Obviously, no single set of rules makes sense in all cases—you must discover what is right for you in your particular situation. In the event that you desire something different out of the relationship than what your co-worker wants, it is important that you make your feelings clear to him.

Avoiding the issue of attraction is likely to have negative consequences. To pretend that attraction will not occur is to leave yourself unprepared when it does. Ensuring that it does not happen by keeping all relationships distant cuts you off from the benefits of close work relationships. Ignoring it once it has developed will result in negative consequences that could have been prevented. It is more useful to anticipate that attraction will develop and to think through how to use it productively.

Needs in Relationships

Your relationships outside work, how far you have progressed in your career, your position in the organization, and your occupation may all affect the kinds of emotional needs you bring to your relationships with co-workers. This is even more the case when male-female attraction is involved. A simple, yet profound example of what we mean can be seen in the contrast between a happily married person and one whose marriage is a source of pain. These two people would be expected to bring strikingly different needs to their relationships in the workplace.

If you are launching a career and, therefore, seeking mentors, sponsors, and contacts, you will have different needs in work relationships than if you are in mid-career and consolidating coalitions for an ascent to the top, or in the later stages of your career and oriented toward assisting other people in their careers.

Similarly, the position you occupy in an organization is significant. Sue, for example, needed relationships in other parts of the company to rescue her from the stagnation she was experiencing. Position in the organizational hierarchy, informal networks in the organization, and length of time with the organization may all affect the needs you bring to your relationships.

Finally, the nature of the work you do and the circumstances under which you do it may influence what you seek from your relationships. For example, individuals whose work focuses on human and emotional issues (such as people in human services or human resources work) may be more inclined to create close relationships with co-workers, as may people doing very demanding and intense work together.

It should be clear, then, that the needs shaping and influencing our relationships are the manifestations of a number of complexly interwoven emotional forces, some of them (for lack of a better word) romantic and others not. You would do well to take a close look at your network of friends and acquaintances, both inside and outside work, to determine what your true needs and objectives are and whether they are being met. It may be that you will be able to fulfill both your professional and personal needs by pursuing closer relationships at work. Conversely, you may decide that your own psychological makeup or the environment at work obliges you to seek relationships outside the office. Or the answer might lie somewhere in between, with some needs being met at work and others outside. The more honest and objective you are with yourself, the more control you will have in managing your relationships.

Interpersonal Competence

The comfort and ability that you have in dealing face to face with complex interpersonal situations will influence how much closeness (or distance) you desire and what you will do to get it. Interaction skills will help to determine whether you get what you intend from your relationships with co-workers of the other sex. Such skills, important in any relationship, are even more crucial in the relationships we are talking about here, in which the risks and the complexity are increased by the joining of personal and professional lives.

In particular, the abilities to listen, empathize, be assertive, and discuss personal and emotional issues are important. These skills are crucial to being able to develop a close relationship with another person and just as significant in being able to increase the distance in a relationship when necessary.

There are a wide variety of educational, training, and therapeutic options available to help you develop the ability to get what you seek from your interpersonal relationships. Such opportunities range from one- or two-hour continuing education introductions to assertiveness or listening, through day- or week-long seminars on leadership skills offered by training staff within companies, through college courses on interpersonal relations, to an ongoing involvement with a therapist.

Forces in the Interaction between You and Another Person

Let's assume you feel attracted to a co-worker. How often, where, and about what you and the other person interact are extremely important factors to consider in trying to manage that attraction. So, too, are the roles you play toward each other and your communication styles. As we look at each of these factors, it is important that we be aware of the effect they have on outsiders' perceptions. People observing a relationship pay close attention to the way you interact for clues to the nature of that relationship. Their conclusions may not always be accurate, but their beliefs are more important than reality in determining their reactions. It may not be fair for co-workers to behave as if there were a romantic relationship when none exists, but people act in relation to the world they see, not to some absolute reality.

Frequency, Setting, and Topics of Interaction

Research in the behavioral sciences has shown that the more two people interact, the more positive their relationship tends to become. To some extent, the design of your work as established by the or-

ganization will determine how much you interact with co-workers—
we'll come back to this later. In addition, you will make choices,
based in part on some of the personal factors discussed earlier,
about how often you wish to interact with particular co-workers.
As relationships develop, however, such choices become an *interpersonal* matter, negotiated explicitly or implicitly and decided on
jointly more than individually. In Sue and Doug's case, for example,
their shared concern about the deteriorating situation within the
work team became the impetus for more frequent meetings, which
doubtless contributed to the development of their own relationship.
Decisions about how often to interact have a clear impact on how
far the relationship develops, what directions it takes, and how
others react to it. By increasing the frequency of your meetings, you
almost certainly increase the likelihood that your conversations will
go beyond work concerns and move into more personal, even intimate, matters. This, as we've said, can be a bad or a good thing,
depending on a host of factors. But it is equally likely that the more
you are seen with a particular co-worker, the more interested, concerned, or even threatened others will become.

   Where you and your co-worker choose to interact (or the places
that are chosen for you) can also affect how the relationship develops
and what impact it has. Of particular significance are atypical settings: off-site, after hours, isolated, social. Significant moments in the
deepening of a relationship often occur in such settings. Sue and
Doug's relationship, for example, went from friendly to romantic
over dinner on a Friday night. Often the setting is not one chosen by
the people themselves. As more and more women enter the work
force and attain higher levels in their companies, they find themselves
more frequently required to travel to branch offices, meetings, and so
on. Away from home, people often relax the barriers that usually
keep the ways they act—and interact—more formal.

   Similarly, the reactions of others can be strongly affected by
where they see you interacting. It is more likely that colleagues will
think you and a co-worker are romantically involved if they see you
eating dinner together at a restaurant than if you are observed having lunch together in the company cafeteria. When travel is involved,
the issue becomes even more complicated—the marital status of the
traveling individuals will certainly provoke comment back at the

office. If your job or career goals require that you spend time on the road, there's not much you can do about it, short of changing jobs or careers. Still, the more aware you are of the messages your own actions convey to your peers and the many factors involved in workplace attractions, the better you will be able to control the situation.

As with frequency of interaction, your decisions about *what* you will discuss with a co-worker become less individual and more interpersonal as the relationship develops. You may find yourself talking about matters raised by the other person that you never would have raised yourself. Topics that make you and your co-worker more vulnerable to each other seem to increase the likelihood of attraction. Of particular significance are discussions of nonwork or personal issues and of the relationship itself, which seem not only to increase intimacy, but also, if overheard, increase the chances that outsiders will believe the relationship is worth gossiping about.

You can influence all three of these aspects of interpersonal interaction. You can increase closeness or distance to a co-worker through careful attention to frequency, location, and topics of interaction. It is also crucial, however, to recognize that these components are greatly influenced by other forces. Relationships take on a life of their own that can carry you along almost without your knowing. Greater consciousness of the way frequency, setting, and topics of interaction are acting to develop or prevent relationships can lead to more satisfactory relationships.

A particularly difficult problem is how to handle a situation in which you are attracted romantically to a co-worker but don't want to let a romantic relationship develop. It has been suggested that airing the subject might reduce the tension in the relationship and defuse the romantic feelings. But some people experience such a conversation as an intimate experience that actually intensifies the romantic inclinations or gives the other person permission to apply pressure for a romantic involvement. If you fear intensification of the feelings, it might be safer to discuss the issue with a friend rather than with the co-worker. Of course, you can also choose not to discuss your attraction with anybody, but the volatility of such feelings may make them difficult to hide.

Roles

In a relationship that lasts any length of time, you and the other person will play various roles in relation to each other. You come to expect certain patterns of behavior from each other, and usually these behaviors do occur.

Sometimes you and the other person design the roles you play with each other especially for your relationship. At other times the *formal* roles each of you plays in the organization are strong determinants of the roles you adopt in relation to each other. For example, a relationship that develops between a supervisor and a secretary is likely to be quite different from a relationship between two department heads. In the first case, the supervisor's formal power over the secretary may represent both a source of attraction and a threat to the latter. The formal power of the department heads, in contrast, is equal (although their informal power may be quite unequal). Their relationship is structured by their formal roles to be much more balanced.

Sometimes you and the other person adopt ready-made roles, particularly if you are uncomfortable in the relationship. For instance, men and women have sometimes tried to manage the uncertainties of working together as peers by putting women in roles consistent with those associated with women outside of work—mother, seductress, cheerleader.

The specific roles you take on can significantly influence the character of the relationship. Taking on ready-made roles, for example, may feel familiar and comfortable but may also limit the potential of the relationship. If a man and woman develop a mentor-protégée relationship, they may well struggle to understand and manage the attraction that often develops through the intense and personal work they do together.

You need to examine the roles you and the other person in a relationship are playing. If you discover that the roles are impeding the development of the type of relationship you desire—and thus, perhaps, your career—or are leading to unwanted assumptions or perceptions by outsiders, some changes may be necessary. You may be able to change roles through direct discussion and negotiation with the other person. Alternatively, you can simply begin to behave differently to demonstrate the new role you desire, although the other person may resist your surprising new behavior.

Communication Processes

Finally, the ways in which you communicate with the other person, both verbally and nonverbally, can influence how your relationship develops and how others react to it. Men and women may unknowingly communicate in nonverbal ways that were learned in the context of their courtship. For example, prolonged eye contact, touching, fixing your hair, and straightening your clothes have been found to be courting cues that men and women may also use in normal work conversation. The potential effects on attraction are obvious. Sensitivity to the nuances of nonverbal communications is not easy to develop, but managing male-female attraction effectively requires that you develop an awareness of how it can complicate interactions.

The verbal component of communication is easier to examine. It's worth thinking about how your words affect your relationships. For example, some people describe teasing, flirting, and using pet names as ways of increasing attraction in a relationship; others regard them as harmless ways of limiting attraction. In either case, they are usually perceived by outsiders as indications of an intimacy that is worthy of investigation.

Forces in the Work Group

As we've said, outsiders will look at the way you and a co-worker interact for cues about the nature of your relationship. The sense that outsiders make of the interactions depends not only on what they observe and their individual ways of seeing the world, but also on the characteristics of the work group (or groups) to which you and the other person belong. Of particular significance are: (1) the unwritten rules of the group, (2) the cohesiveness of the group, and (3) the roles you and the other person play in the group.

Unwritten Rules

It is possible that the unwritten rules of the group could encourage attraction. Work groups may wish to create mother and father figures or to support the potential for creativity represented by a male-female pair. Most evidence suggests, however, that groups seek to prevent pairing off. The competition for energy and loyalty that an intense two-person relationship could evoke often concerns and threatens the other people in the group. Similarly, if you pair off with someone from another group, issues of security and confidentiality may develop. Such concerns are probably greater at higher levels of the organization, where the people involved have more control over resources and decision making and, therefore, greater potential for damage exists.

If the people in a group think you are involved in an intimate relationship with one of its members—or with a co-worker outside the group—they are likely to act to prevent the disruption of the familiar group dynamics. The cool reception Sue Bredbeck received from the project team and her subsequent unhappy experiences with them demonstrated these group forces in action.

Cohesiveness

Closely related to the influence of a group's unwritten rules is its level of cohesiveness. The more close-knit a group is, the more powerful its unwritten rules are and the more influence it has on all the people who make up the group, including you. A closely knit group derives its power from the strong feelings of belonging it offers and the desire of people to remain part of a socially satisfying entity. The reactions of a highly cohesive group to a potential or perceived relationship are likely to be more intense than those of a less cohesive group—and the pressures you feel will be correspondingly more intense. It is also important to note, however, that cohesiveness in a group means, by definition, the presence of positive emotions. The cohesive group thus can serve as a breeding ground for male-female attractions. You may be brought together with another person within the group and then discouraged by the group from getting too involved.

The power Doug's team possessed in relation to Sue and Doug had much to do with its cohesiveness. Doug already felt a part of a group he described as friendly and very sociable, and Sue undoubtedly anticipated becoming a member of this highly attractive unit.

Their negative reactions to Sue and then to Doug were, therefore, much more powerful than they might have been in a less cohesive setting.

Roles

The roles you and the other person adopt toward each other in a relationshp have already been discussed. Both of you also play roles in your work group(s). The most significant role within a group is that of the leader, whether formal or informal. The people in a group may feel particularly threatened if a relationship or potential relationship involves the leader. They may fear that access to the leader will be impeded or that the leader will no longer manage the resources of the group equitably. They also may be concerned about the leader's reputation and effectiveness in managing the group's relationships with other departments and important people outside the group.

Sue and Doug probably faced more intense negative reactions from other people on the team because of Doug's special position as team leader. The familiar dynamics between group members and the group leader were threatened by the entry of a woman who others in the group feared might distract him and cloud his judgment.

A solo woman in an otherwise all-male work group may experience a very rocky road. It wll be particularly noticeable if she is attracted to or attractive to a man in the group. She may be perceived as a scarce resource by others and punished more severely for any pairing attempts.

In failing to see their relationship from the perspective of the group, Sue and Doug did not appreciate the threat they represented. The first step in managing such a relationship, then, is to assess the social dynamics of the group realistically.

Resist the temptation to hide the relationship from the group(s). It is almost impossible. No information travels as quickly through an organizational grapevine than news of an intramural romance. Instead, try to reassure the other people in the group. If the personality of the group supports it, an open discussion about what the relationship could mean to everyone involved might reduce anxieties. Such a discussion could take place with the group as a whole or with individual members. Build in methods of assuring people in the group that no one will be compromised by the relationship. This can be done by establishing independent checks on key decisions and performance.

Forces in the Organization

You and all your work relationships—romantic, group, and so on—are embedded in the organization for which you work. Its formal structures, its policies and procedures, its informal or unwritten rules and regulations, and the people who communicate and enforce them all affect the development and management of male-female attraction.

The Formal Organization

Your organization's job design (the way work is organized); its reward system (pay, promotion, perks, vacation, recognition, and so on); and its performance management system (performance appraisal, employee training programs, career development programs) all have a significant impact on male-female attraction.

Job design directly affects the opportunities for people to interact in the workplace. For example, when project teams are used to get work done (as in Doug's new product team), men and women have more task-related reasons to interact. As a result, they will be more likely to develop relationships than when work is organized into individualized tasks that require little interaction with others. By the same token, however, it should be kept in mind that frequent interaction also means that everyone's actions affect everyone else in the group. The consequences of attraction are magnified in a group setting. Sue and Doug's relationship probably would have been less significant if it had not occurred in the context of a group working on highly interconnected tasks.

The reward system affects people's behavior at work in general, and their behavior in relationships in particular. The extent to which an organization rewards managers for developing their employees, and everyone for establishing good working relationships, appears to affect people's inclinations to become involved in relationships. When only bottom-line results are rewarded, devoting time and energy to relationships may be seen as risky, a distraction from what really counts. Another important reward system issue is how the organization responds to sexual harassment—the misuse of male-female work relationships. If the organization does not punish those who harass, people in low-power positions will be likely to keep their distance in potential relationships.

A final aspect of the formal organization that can affect male-female relationships is the performance management system. Relationships can develop during performance appraisals, career development programs, and employee training and development as people interact with co-workers about important personal and professional issues. The performance management system provides a setting in which male-female attraction can naturally emerge.

You face significant challenges if you attempt to get the formal organization to change. The situation, however, may not be as bleak as it first appears. These formal components are probably more easily altered than are such things as the informal systems we will discuss next, the unwritten rules of groups, or the attitudes and beliefs of individuals. New job designs can be developed, training programs can be instituted, reward systems can be restructured. The specific means by which this can be done obviously depend on your organization and your place in it. The changes should be oriented toward facilitating rich and rewarding relationships among women and men working together, consistent with excellent organizational performance. Needless restrictions on the natural attractions co-workers will feel toward each other should be eliminated. For example, policies that forbid employees from dating each other often push such behavior underground and make the resulting dynamics more complex.

The Informal Organization

Although you may wish to change the formal organization, understanding the informal organization is probably the most you can hope for. An organization's culture—its shared values, informal rules, rites, rituals—is rich, complex, and elusive. Nonetheless, you need to make the effort to understand it because the culture significantly affects your relationships with co-workers.

The informal organization communicates powerful messages about what behavior is appropriate. For example, in company A, where traditional sex-role stereotypes dominate the organizational culture, people report that it is quite risky for male and female co-workers to be seen at lunch or after work together. The rumor mill labels such informal interaction inappropriate, and careers can be damaged. As a consequence, women and men avoid each other and relationships do not develop. In company B, on the other hand, where the impact of traditional sex-role stereotypes has diminished, the threat of the rumor mill still exists to some extent, but women and men interact much more freely, providing the opportunity for attraction to develop.

These unwritten messages from the informal organization sometimes reinforce the influence of a particular group's unwritten rules. Other times, the culture of the organization will communicate very different expectations.

Your challenge is to read the informal organization as you attempt to manage male-female attraction. Paying attention to such things as the stories that are told about men and women working together, the way the grapevine works, and the things that make people visible or invisible in the organization can help you decide how to handle your attractions at work.

Leaders' Behavior

Leaders' behaviors can shape members' interest and level of comfort in building relationships. If, for example, the male leaders of an organization serve as models of effective coaching, mutual respect, friendship, and good rapport with women in the organization, and if they openly endorse policy changes and educational programs that enable women and men to work together effectively, it will encourage and support the development of relationships between women and men in the organization.

In contrast, if leaders support education and policy changes on paper, but their behavior is a different story, or if both women and men perceive that the men at the top are not comfortable working with competent women, or if rumors about senior male managers having sexual liaisons with female subordinates cause hostility and resentment, it will obviously make the development of constructive male-female work relationships less likely.

The leaders' reactions to male-female relationships that do develop are also very important. Doug's boss's handling of the rumored romance did not increase the chances that that relationship would have positive consequences. Other people will watch closely to see how the leaders deal with such relationships for cues as to how to behave.

You can begin by observing the behaviors of your organization's leaders as part of your effort to read the organizational culture. But you may be able to go beyond that. If you think your bosses can handle such issues, you can ask for help from at least your direct boss in the potentially problematic relationships.

Sue Bredbeck Revisited

Let's return to Sue Bredbeck's situation to see how an understanding of the forces that affect attraction can be used to manage such situations more effectively.

Sue might have spared herself some pain if she had examined closely her own attitudes toward relationships with co-workers of the other sex. Although she seemed to possess a healthy openness to becoming attracted to co-workers, she also seemed to assume, somewhat naively, that she could pursue such attractions without worrying about others' reactions. Only after the relationship had become romantic did Sue realize that such a step might have significant career implications. A careful look at her own attitudes and beliefs before ever being faced with the possibility of a relationship and a continuing reexamination as the events unfolded might have allowed her to manage the reality of a relationship more effectively.

Sue might also have been able to handle the situation more effectively if she had considered the likely reactions of others to the frequency and settings of her interactions with Doug. Probably she was rumored to be romantically involved with Doug long before it was true. Had she been aware of the cues she and Doug were giving to outsiders, she might have been much more concerned about her relationship with those people.

If Sue had recognized that a male-female pair can represent a significant threat to a group, she might have avoided some of the unpleasantness she experienced. She and Doug might have worked to reduce the threat and reassure the group.

Sue can now use the reactions of the woman from the Human Resources Department and Doug's boss as valuable information about the organization's informal rules regarding romance between co-workers. Karen Boyer's reaction suggests some sophistication regarding the complexity of the issues facing Sue and Doug. Doug's boss, on the other hand, is obviously very uncomfortable with the possibility of a romance between two of his employees. (One wonders whether his organization had provided clear guidelines on the subject of what is acceptable and what is not. Had any of the managers in the company been trained on how to handle the sensitive issue of sexual attraction in the office?) Sue needs to put this information in the context of the other information she has about the organization to develop her strategy for managing the relationship from here.

You can manage your attractions at work more effectively if you are aware of the complex set of forces that can cause potentially constructive relationships to do damage to you, your co-workers, and your organization. Attraction between men and women at work will continue to increase. Whether it will be a source of creativity, productivity, and development or of conflict, disruption, and pain will depend on your ability to manage the complexities effectively yourself and infuence your organization to become a setting in which people can interact productively.

References

Bradford, D.L.; Sargent, A.G.; and Sprague, M.S. 1975. "The Executive Man and Woman: The Issue of Sexuality." In F.E. Gordon and M.H. Strober, eds., *Bringing Women into Management*. New York: McGraw-Hill.

Clawson, J.G., and Kram, K.E. 1984. "Managing Cross-Gender Mentoring." *Business Horizons* 27 (3):22–32.

Collins, E.G.C., 1983. "Managers and Lovers." *Harvard Business Review* 61 (5):142–153.

Fitt, L.W., and Newton, D.A. 1981. "When the Mentor Is a Man and The Protégée a Woman." *Harvard Business Review* 59 (2):56–60.

Jamison, K. 1983. "Managing Sexual Attraction in the Workplace." *Personnel Administrator*, August.

Josefowitz, N. 1982. "Sexual Relationships at Work: Attraction, Transference, Coercion, or Strategy." *Personnel Administrator* 27 (3):91–96.

Kram, K.E. 1985. *Mentoring at Work: Developmental Relationships in Organizational Life*. Glenview, Ill.: Scott, Foresman.

Quinn, R.E., 1977. "Coping with Cupid: The Formation, Impact, and Management of Romantic Relationships in Organizations." *Administrative Science Quarterly* 22 (March):30–45.

6
Women as Bosses: Helping with the Transition

Natasha Josefowitz

Women in the work force. They face very different dynamics than men do by the mere fact of their sex. What can *they* do to get integrated? What can management do to help this process? Being in transition means being between two chairs. You have left the comfortable seat that is familiar to you, but you don't yet have another chair to sit on. A new workplace or a new position is like sitting between two chairs. The memory of the old one is still very much present, but the old chair is not there anymore, and the new one is still unfamiliar. What are some of the more common situations in which women find themselves, and what can they do to ease the transition?

We will look at the following possibilities:

A promotion from the ranks from worker to supervisor, so that you have to deal with former friends and co-workers who are now subordinates.

A promotion into a male-dominated workplace where you have to manage sexist co-workers.

A transfer from another department, which means being new and not new at the same time.

Some of this material has been excerpted from the author's new book, *You're the Boss: A Guide to Managing People with Understanding and Effectiveness* (New York: Warner Books, 1985). © 1985 by Natasha Josefowitz. All rights reserved. Used by permission.

Being hired from the outside—having to earn one's stripes, pass muster, and pay one's dues.

If some of the possible reactions from the woman herself, her peers, her subordinates, and her bosses can be anticipated, then they can be handled better than if they come as a surprise and often as a shock.

Any transition to a new job or a new position involves first impressions—the impression the woman makes on others and the impression others make on her. Studies have shown that these early impressions last longer than one would suspect.[1] As weeks, months, and even years pass, those early memories of the people and climate at one's workplace may remain fixed, even though the environment has changed or the people act very differently than they did at the beginning. That first impression a woman makes in the first hour, day, week; that first meeting where she speaks up (or doesn't); that first project she works on with her peers; that first encounter with a subordinate or with her boss—these will remain in people's minds more vividly than her subsequent actions for a long, long time. Yet very little attention is paid to those transitions: the first minutes after a promotion, the first hour after a new manager has been hired, the first words exchanged, the first actions performed.

Let's suppose you're a woman who has just been promoted from the ranks after many years with the company. You probably think you've been there long enough to know the ropes. In many ways you do, but in some ways you don't. You have never belonged to the management team and have not operated from that perspective. What pitfalls you should anticipate, and what are some of the benefits and rewards you can expect from the job?

Even though you know everything there is to know about your organization, your department, and your workers, from the day you are promoted everything changes. You will now be perceived differently, you will be talked to differently, and your former colleagues will wait to see if you will change. And you *will* change. If you don't, you will not be doing your job. Your relationships based on years of friendship and years of sharing daily events will not be the same. You are now in a position of authority, and you can affect the lives of others. Some of those others will be political opportunists. They'll stay on your good side, and they'll try to use the friendship to their advantage. You'll get requests like this:

You don't mind if I take Friday off, do you?

You're going to report *that* after what *we* used to do?

Oh, come on, let me leave a little earlier; what's with the new boss stuff?

I really want to go to the game my kid is in, how about not reporting me absent?

What's the matter with you? You've turned into a drill sargeant or something.

It will be difficult to establish your role because you can no longer indulge in old patterns of behavior—sharing secrets or gossiping about your supervisors, covering for one another, or taking longer lunches with former peers who are now your subordinates—because you will then be seen as playing favorites.

You are not the person you were yesterday; you are a boss, and being a boss is a role. A role is a prescription for behavior, and you now have a new prescription. As soon as you step into your new job, you're in the role of a supervisor. This does not mean being phony. You bring who you are to that role. You may not want to accept this; you may wonder: "Why do I need to change? Why do I have to give up the easy sociability?" If you don't revise your social behavior, however, you will face an impossible task when you must refuse favors or reprimand, discipline, demote, or even fire people who are your friends. This does not mean that you are no longer a friend but that you're a boss first. You cannot choose to remain equal, for you are not. You now have power. You can influence others' lives, and they know it. You will be treated differently; the change may be subtle, but the nonverbal cues are there. Are your former peers a bit more deferential, are you being observed more closely, does your opinion matter more, have you become the topic of conversation, do people speculate on your motives or your next moves? If you continue to act as if you were still a peer, you may be liked but not respected. If you choose to accept your dominant position, you may lose the pleasant camaraderie but will earn respect if you are a fair boss.

This is not an easy choice, but it must be made at the start. Your workers will be watching you closely to see what you do. Don't count on their making it easy for you; it is to their advantage to keep you at their level. There are some exceptions: when group work is effective without formal leadership, or when workers can begin their jobs on their own and can control their own results, you, the supervisor, though still accountable to higher-ups, may be more of a team member than a leader. More often than not, however, this won't happen.

Let's take an example. Nora had been in sales for many years. She liked her job, the income it produced, and especially the friends she had at work. Families got together for picnics, couples went bowling, women babysat for each other. Company policy had been to promote from within, but even though she had seniority, the managers had always been men. Finally, Nora was promoted. Naturally she was pleased; her boss assured her she would have no trouble because she knew the organization and the people so well. Nora's friends congratulated her, saying that finally "one of us made it." But was she still one of them? Nora received more invitations to come by for coffee and dessert in one week than she had in the previous six months. Nancy, her closest friend, had already asked to be switched to another part of the department. What should she do?

If Nora is smart, she'll tell Nancy she can't play favorites, explaining that she would appear unfair to the others and adding that if an opportunity arises where the switch will make sense, she'll remember her request. Nora faces a difficult time, when she'll have to make some tough choices between remaining a friend or being a fair boss. The change of role from worker to supervisor may be the most difficult adjustment in the workplace, especially for women who have been brought up to value relationships, friendships, and support.[2]

The exciting thing about being in a position of influence is that you can make a difference in the lives of your workers; you can now do some of the things you wish would have been done for you when you were one of them. However, you must be very careful not to overstep boundaries. What seemed like a reasonable request when you were a worker may not be productive in terms of management. You need to check with your boss before you make any decisions that affect your workers to be sure you have a management perspective and not an employee one. For instance, as an employee you may have balked at having to use old equipment, but as a manager you understand the budgetary constraints and may have decided that bigger bonuses will be more rewarding than the latest hardware. This does not mean you are not sympathetic to the needs of your subordinates. Who knows better than you what will create a better work climate? Take advantage of your knowledge, but be careful about your primary identity. It is not as a worker, but as a manager. What makes it so difficult to feel like management is that you still have a support group with your former peers but have not yet acquired one with your new ones. Sitting between two chairs is always very uncomfortable. It will remain so for a while.

How can management help a woman in this situation? The first way, and probably the most important, is to provide her with support. This must come from two sources: her own boss, who should be sympathetic, and her new colleagues, who should be helped to make her feel welcome in their midst. By being available to her, by introducing her to the others, by including her in informal gatherings, by giving her opportunities to show what she can do, they can make her credibility and acceptance easier.

Let's take a different situation. Suppose you are a woman who has been recently hired, and you have done your job really well—in fact, better than others who have been there longer. Suppose you are also younger than the rest, yet your boss just promoted you. Because you still feel fairly new, you may feel the promotion is coming too soon—that you haven't had a chance to learn all you need to know about your job.

You may wonder—is it because you worked hard, because you're smart, or because of affirmative action? Does the company need to fill a slot or fulfill a quota? You may not feel prepared; you are probably scared. Many people assume they're not ready, or they're not good enough, or they'll be found out. Women make this assumption more often than men do. (Research indicates that college men with a C+ average think they can do graduate work, but college women with a B+ average think they cannot.)

You may feel like a learner, and in many ways you are. But as long as you perceive yourself as a novice, you give that impression to others—and the impression may last longer than you wish. Don't be afraid to make mistakes. Few errors are irreparable; your first few mistakes are part of your training. Only fearful people never make mistakes, because they do nothing. You probably have higher expectations of yourself than anyone else has. What you don't know, you will learn on the job. Remember, if you do something wrong, *you* are not the mistake, and the mistake is only *a* mistake. Women more often than men seem to blame themselves for their errors. Men more often blame others or outside circumstances for their mistakes and avoid feeling guilty about the negative outcome.

You have two points of view to consider: how you perceive yourself and how others perceive you. If you think of yourself as inadequate, unready, too young, too new, too junior, you will project this image by the way you stand, sit, talk, and even dress. You can come across either as a helpless young thing who doesn't know anything or as a person who accepts responsibilities and who can ask for whatever information you need to perform effectively or can seek the necessary training.

Don't wait until you think you've asked all the questions, mastered all the techniques, and done all the research. Begin having authority from day one. First impressions last. In some organizations, if you give the impression that you are a learner, you will always be remembered as a learner and will have a hard time transcending that image.

This brings us to the second problem: how others perceive you. If some people think you have been promoted too quickly, you may be resented for quite a while: why her and not me? If you were a man, some people would accuse you of having pull or using friendships to get ahead. Since you're a woman, men who have been passed over may say you've benefited unfairly from affirmative action and may be angry at you for taking advantage of a political situation. Other women who may have less merit than you may attribute your promotion to the fact that you flirted with your boss. They may hint that you are apple-polishing or sleeping your way to the top. It is often comforting for the one who has been passed over to believe that someone has done well not because she's better, but because of some unfair advantage she has used for her own advancement, such as political or sexual manipulation. Seldom if ever will someone say, "She has more qualified than I am and will do a better job than I could have." It is human nature to protect one's ego.

This doesn't mean that some people might not be genuinely pleased for you and ready to cooperate. But others will be competitive and difficult to work with; they may even try to sabotage you by spreading gossip, not cooperating with others, or not producing quality products or services. None of this should frighten you away; it is a worst-case scenario. If everything always went smoothly, there would be no need to write about it.

Sandra had been working a short time as a researcher in the chemical lab of a large drug company when her boss called her in and asked her if she would like to be in charge of a seven-person lab, the present supervisor of which was being transferred. Sandra was surprised; she had only recently received her advanced degree, but she knew her work was exceptional. She worried what others would say, especially the two older men who were continually denigrating her. Her boss felt she was the most creative member of the team in addition to being very meticulous and committed to doing well. Often she would work late into the night rather than stopping in the middle of an experiment. When she mentioned her concern about being accepted by her peers, her boss just shrugged his shoulders. Sandra asked him to make the announcement and to be very clear about her new responsibilities. Sandra was right to be uncomfortable: there was much grumbling, often within earshot. She decided to sit down with the members of the team and discuss the various projects they were working on, her expectations, their problems, and her willingness to be supportive. With the support of her boss, she was able to confront the more difficult men with their feelings about having a younger female in charge. Mike, the oldest member of the team, gave her the most trouble. He talked disparagingly about women in general and was barely polite to her. Although Sandra was afraid of a confrontation, she felt one was necessary. She asked him to come to her office and, in front of Mike, asked her secretary to hold all calls. Note her strategy in the following conversation:

Sandra: Mike, you seem particularly unhappy with my promotion. Is it because of something I have done, because you worry I won't work out, or just because I'm a woman and you don't believe women should be in charge? [Notice that she offers him alternative explanations for his behavior.]

Mike: Well, I just don't understand why the boss thinks you're so great. We never had a woman doing this kind of work, and I don't know why we should start now.

Sandra: In other words, you're not sure I'm going to be good, and you're
worried about the future of the lab. [She offers him a face-saving device.]

Mike: Right, you haven't proved yourself, and there's so much at stake.

Sandra: I appreciate your concern, and I wish everyone cared as much as
you do. I think you should trust the boss's judgment—he believes I can
do the job. I also hope you'll give me a chance to prove myself. I want
this lab to do well just as much as you do, so we share this, but I need
your help, Mike. You're competent, and you have a lot of experience.
Suppose you tell me when you see any signs of problems, and we can
talk about them. I know it's hard for a lot of men to work with a
woman. [She does not say, work *for* me, or *for* a woman, but *with* a
woman.]

Mike: Well, I don't know, we'll see.

Sandra: Will you give us both a chance to work together?

Mike: I guess so.

Sandra's efforts paid off. She became accepted because of her
competence as a chemist, and even more because of her sensitivity
and courage in dealing with difficult issues, thus proving her competence as a manager.

How can she be helped to feel comfortable as a new boss? First,
by having her own boss really believe she is at least as well, if not
better, qualified than the others, and by having this belief made
known to her subordinates and colleagues in order to dispel any
fantasies they may have about affirmative action goals. This woman
will need visible support from management. She may also need
training for her new role. This may be done in house or by enrolling
her in management training seminars and workshops. Often qualified women are given opportunities for advancement but no help in
making that transition.

Let us consider another type of situation. This one concerns
either a lateral move from one department to another, or a promotion from one part of the organization to another. In either case the
issues are the same: you are both an old hand and a newcomer at the
same time.

Although you may know the organization well, you probably
have only a vague notion of who your colleagues and subordinates
are, what they do, or what is expected of them. This is a treacherous

situation, because the tendency will be to do things as they were done in your former workplace, which may not fit the needs of the new place. Information and misinformation about you may have preceded your entry. You, too, may have gathered impressions from hearsay or previous contact with the people that may or may not be correct. You must check it out for yourself. Entering a new position is like getting married: it's a matter of fit. Everything depends on how the people involved work out their specific differences among themselves; the important issue is the relationship between you and your peers and subordinates. We all change for better or worse depending on whom we're with; your workers will behave differently depending on who their colleagues and bosses are.

Moving from one department to another provides an opportunity to learn the norms (the unwritten rules) from scratch. Within the same organization, one unit may be sexist, having never had a female boss before; another may have had good experiences with female workers, so that a female boss is not an issue.

Just as workers will want to see the same patterns repeated (there is security in the familiar), so you, as a new boss, will have a tendency to manage as your former boss did; you will do things that worked in your other department. It is crucial to observe, take stock, and learn about the new place and new position, using newness to your advantage by asking questions that can only really be asked at the beginning of a new job. You should be willing to do some things *their* way instead of *your* way, or to compromise, for people are most committed to doing their work well if they can participate in the decisions that affect their jobs.

You may be expected to know specific things that in fact you do not know, such as interviewing or running effective meetings. Yet there are many things that would normally take years to find out with which you are already familiar, such as the idiosyncrasies of the individual workers or the history of the company. In being transferred and/or promoted, you have the best and the worst of all possible worlds.

Susan moved only two floors down, but what a difference in the work climate! For example, in her old department the coffee break was scheduled and observed from 10:00 A.M. to 10:15 A.M.; in the new department, it was somewhere between 10:00 A.M. and 11:00 A.M.

(more or less ten to twenty minutes), and no one seemed to care either way. Susan knew that if she were to institute a rigid fifteen-minute break, she would make people angry, so she decided to see if people would take advantage of a flexible break and whether it would reduce productivity. She thought if the time taken off were to stretch too often to thirty minutes, she would say that fifteen minutes was all that was allowed, but that it could be taken anytime between 10:00 A.M. and 10:30 A.M., thus offering some flexibility within a more rigid time span. Susan was prepared to go along with the norms as long as they were not unproductive. She also had a plan ready in case she needed an alternative. As it happened, she was tested only once, by an employee who did take a long break—thirty-five minutes. She spoke to the worker, reminding him not to take advantage of the flexibility, and the offense was not repeated. Susan had set the limits not only for that one subordinate but also for all the others who were waiting to see how she would react.

How can management help? By providing her with information about her predecessor. It is important for the transferred woman not to assume she already knows all about her new area. She should observe who does what, how, when, with what consequences, and for whom; she should find out what kind of a boss was there before her and how he or she did things, and whether or not it was satisfactory to the employees. If the previous boss was very much liked and is now missed, she'll have a harder time because she'll be expected to fit someone else's style, which is impossible. She can deal with this situation by being up front about it; she can say that she has heard how wonderful the former boss was and that she hopes to do as well, but that everyone's way of managing is different. On the other hand, if the former boss was ineffective or disliked, subordinates may have unrealistic expectations that the new boss will save the situation. Unless she is informed about the history and the politics of the particular unit or department, she will have a harder time helping her workers adjust their expectations to ones that are reasonable, and both she and they could face serious disappointment or even failure.

We come now to our final example: Suppose you, as a new female supervisor, have been hired from another company. You have a good track record, are an expert in your field, and have an advanced degree. But how will you fit in?

The first rule is to not expect perfection from yourself or anyone else; let the work proceed as it has been, observe, and make notes on what you see or hear. Make a list of your workers and note what they do; study their job descriptions. Do they actually do what their job descriptions say they do? Do they do more, less, or something entirely different? Are they productive, and do they seem content? List the patterns you observe. Who comes in early or leaves late? Who socializes with whom? How hard do individuals work? What is the mood in the office? Is the work boring or challenging? Study file records, turnover rates, absenteeism, sick leaves, and complaints. In other words, do what an anthropologist does in an alien culture: study the ways of the inhabitants. Little by little, you will begin to make sense of their culture. Establish a relationship with your employees: talk, ask questions, get a feeling for their weaknesses and their strengths. Don't make quick judgments or promises. Wait a while before you take action; what may seem disruptive at first may not be in the long run. New managers, eager to show their ability, tend to start making changes too early. Tell your workers you need time to observe and think about what you see, and only then do you plan to make decisions about what will continue as is and what will be changed. If you feel pressure from your own supervisor to perform immediately, ask him or her for the time you need to become better informed.

Joyce had been an assistant buyer for some years and knew the clothing business well. Now, there she was, hired to manage a department in a large appliance discount store. There were hectic periods, when the salespeople bustled about trying to serve impatient customers, and quiet periods, when there seemed to be little for them to do. She noticed that even when there was work to be done during slack times, the salespeople stood around chatting and then, as soon as customers came in, sprang into action. She thought of changing this and assigning tasks, but decided to wait and see. She was right. Salespeople were active when they needed to be and took a needed rest from the pressure when they could, managing to keep up with the paperwork in between, without having it rigidly scheduled. Had Joyce insisted on setting specific times for the work to be done, she would have run into resistance. The atmosphere was friendly, people helped one another, and the salespeople needed to relax in between their very busy times. Joyce decided to keep observing and to do nothing unless she noticed that work was not being performed adequately.

The anthropological attitude when entering a new job or a new position is always a helpful stance, because it lets the new person be more objective. It's harder to be as analytical when you are promoted from the ranks because it's also your own culture, and it's almost impossible to detach yourself from it enough to pretend to be an outsider looking in.

How can management help? The new female manager needs to know that her boss has confidence in her and saw her potential; she must be told what her boss's expectations are, both immediately and in due time. A new supervisor will learn the nitty-gritty of everyday work from her own boss, but from a higher-up executive she needs to understand the big picture.

The big picture means the total organization. What is the purpose of this company? What are its short-term goals? What are its long-range ones? Where is it going? Is there a value system, such as, "Let's have the best-trained people in the field," or, "Let's get this done the fastest and cheapest way," or, "Let's beat the competition," or, "Be the first," or, "People's problems outside of work are not our business," or, "We're a company who cares?" Even though each organization is basically concerned with overall productivity, the means used to get to that goal represent the company's value system.

It is important to discuss the big picture because the new supervisor tends to identify herself with the workers when she should start identifying with management. She is part of the management team now, and even though she may feel her support comes more from her workers than from her equals or her superiors, she will have to avoid the trap of settling in where she is most comfortable—with her former peers—rather than getting to know her new peers and bosses. This task is made even more difficult because there is a tendency for men in management not to think of the new female manager as a part of their team. They might unconsciously exclude her from both formal and informal meetings and gatherings. It is important for her also to understand *what* the organizational goals are and what means are used to obtain them in order to find out *who* in the organization seems to be fulfilling these expectations best.

Those are the people with power. For example, if the company wants to be in the forefront with new products, innovations will be valued; therefore, the people who are willing to take risks and test new ideas will do better than the conservatives who do things the way they've always been done. If the company is run by older, more careful people, who know a good thing when they have it and prefer to stick with it, a person with bright ideas on how to improve matters will not be welcome. Expectations will also be affected by whether the organization is in a period of growth and expansion, in a period of stability, or in a period of trying to survive by cutting back.

Because there are always tensions in any system, a woman will need political understanding to survive. The balance of power is always changing, so she must keep reading the signs to know what is going on.

At the beginning, it is important for her to try to fit into the mold—to do things the way they have always been done. Only much later, when she has gained credibility and is well established, can she begin to change existing conditions. The way a new supervisor or manager gets started in the system will predict the ease of her transition and subsequent integration and will determine to a large degree her effectiveness as a boss.

In other words, people at higher levels of management can make a difference by understanding what a new woman in the organization is up against from the very beginning and by demonstrating this understanding in the way they welcome the newcomer. Here are some of the more negative, and many times unconscious, ways that women are made to feel less welcome and certainly less effective:

Overprotecting her by holding back criticism or giving her assignments that are too easy.

Excluding her from informal get-togethers.

Calling her by endearing terms.

Drawing her into traditional female roles by selecting her to prepare food, take notes, or copy materials.

Providing solutions rather than allowing her to think things through.

Discrediting her by paraphrasing what she has just said for the benefit of others.

Testing her loyalty by telling her she's not like other women or she thinks like a man.

Going along with other males' sexist remarks, promoting negative attitudes toward affirmative action in the company.[4]

Relationships established at the beginning will be the predictors of future contacts. What is established as a norm at the start will facilitate interactions with supervisors and managers in the coming months and years and, more important, will model the behavior they can have in turn with their subordinates.

Notes

1. J.P. Kotter, "The Psychological Contract: Managing the Joining Up Process," *California Management Review* 15 (1973):91–99.
2. Ellyn Miriades and Andre Cote, "Women in Management: Strategies for Removing the Barriers," *Personnel Administrator*, April 1980.
3. Rosalind Barnett, Wellesley College Center for Research on Women, Wellesley, Mass., June 1980.
4. Adapted from Judith Palmer, "How to Make a Woman Lose Effectiveness in an Organization," in Natasha Josefowitz, ed., *You're the Boss: A Guide to Managing People with Understanding and Effectiveness* (New York: Warner Books, 1985). Reprinted by permission.

7

When Older Women Work for Younger Women

Joanna Henderson
Betty Lou Marple

It was a twist of events Ruthanne Edwards could never have imagined. After spending four years in a graduate program in counseling specifically geared toward women who had been out of the work force for a number of years and could only attend part time, she had finally earned her master's degree. This had come after completing her undergraduate work over the course of six years on a catch-as-catch-can basis. She had taken one course at a time whenever the demands of children and a husband (whose work had required relocation twice in those six years) were relaxed. Having completed her education and partially launched her children, Ruthanne was offered the kind of job she had hoped she could land. As a counselor in a nearby university's continuing education program, she was responsible for helping adults work out academic programs that meshed with their job aspirations. Quite naturally she also became involved with problems centering around time and stress management, reluctant spouses, and children.

Ruthanne felt useful and valued. Her work was interesting, it was flexible enough to accommodate her home life, and it paid far more than she was expecting. After eight weeks on the job, only one nagging doubt continued to plague her. Her boss, a snappy and energetic woman fifteen years younger than Ruthanne and recently graduated with a doctorate from a prestigious school, never seemed to appreciate fully Ruthanne's talents, patience, and ability to listen. Many of these skills came as much from running a busy household as they did from her graduate work in counseling, but they were appreciated by the adult teachers as well as by Ruthanne's counselor peers, all of whom were also younger. Only Sarah, Ruthanne's boss, seemed not to notice and never said anything positive to her.

This would have been acceptable if Sarah had not also begun to take pot shots at Ruthanne's inability to stay late several nights a week. When Ruthanne requested a forty-minute break one afternoon to drive her youngest child and his cohorts to soccer practice because the group had missed the school bus, Sarah blew her celebrated cool. Refraining from any reference to age or familial responsibilities, she nonetheless reminded Ruthanne that the counselors needed her too and that her major responsibilities were to the students in the university. Further, she wondered aloud if Ruthanne really had the energy and stamina to keep up with the job's requirements and more than hinted that Ruthanne might be more comfortable in a part-time situation. There was no mention of good work, no praise for Ruthanne's speedy adjustment to the working environment she had left behind fifteen years earlier. Ruthanne's joy quickly turned to depression, and she began to doubt her own ability to do the job.

The older professional woman who works for the younger woman is an emerging issue. As many educated women return to school, enter second careers, or find new occupations, some of those in middle age find that in order to learn a new set of skills, they need to take jobs at levels where they report to younger, highly educated or trained women. These younger women have not taken time out for family, nor have they trained for traditional female jobs. Instead, they have moved directly into management positions from undergraduate and professional school (often in schools and programs that were closed to women until the early 1970s). They have, in fact, followed the path that male managers have historically pursued.

Ruthanne's story is not unusual. Its uniqueness lies in the fact that it could not have been told fifteen or twenty years ago, when women worked for men and younger people worked for older people. These conventions were strictly honored; they existed as unspoken rules, as strongly obeyed as the rules that said women were secretaries and men were managers. But before we look more closely at this new phenomenon, we need to examine the situation in which Ruthanne Edwards's boss finds herself.

Sarah Heller graduated from Yale, worked for two years in public relations, and then returned to graduate school to pursue more deeply a long-standing interest in psychology. Within three years she had earned a doctorate at Harvard's School of Education. An internship done in her last year at the school in the continuing education division of another nearby university led first to an assistant director's job and then to the position of director. The job was a plum, one for which Sarah might have waited five years had the previous director not decided to return to full-time teaching. And so, having arrived at an early age in a place that Sarah felt she fully deserved because of hard work, good grades at top-notch schools, and a keen eye for seizing opportunities, she suddenly found herself responsible for a staff of twelve and a budget of half a million dollars. Determined to do an outstanding job as the first woman and the youngest person to hold the title, she began by making careful selections for counselors.

When Ruthanne arrived for her interview, Sarah was excited about the possibility of employing a mature professional in the department. Much of the staff were either her own age or only slightly older or younger, but many of the students in the continuing education division were around Ruthanne's age. Ruthanne was hired almost immediately after a quick interview, without either woman addressing aloud the fact that they came from different generations. (Later, each mentioned that she had thought about the age difference but said it had seemed both unprofessional and possibly even illegal to mention it.)

Things never did go smoothly between the two. From the beginning Sarah found that Ruthanne reminded her of her own mother. Ruthanne would straighten Sarah's desk, remind her to drive carefully, and point out that she didn't care for her geraniums properly. "They need to go thoroughly dry between waterings," she said to Sarah one day while looking over the plants after an office meeting. Ruthanne's behavior soon became grating to Sarah. Further, Sarah who had become somewhat of a workaholic in her new position, often worked late and expected her staff to do the same. Ruthanne's unwillingness to do this and her need to leave for short periods during the day from time to time were disruptive to Sarah. The younger woman admitted she did not know how to manage the older woman.

Sarah was threatened, frustrated, and baffled by Ruthanne, all of which caused her to feel she had failed as a supervisor in this situation. She simply was not bringing out the best in a subordinate who had so much to offer. Both women had worked hard to arrive at an ideal place in their respective careers. Both were unhappy. What had gone wrong?

Somebody to Nobody?

Men have always lived with a similar situation; that is exactly what makes the problem for women so different. In earlier days, when the economy was more closely tied to the land, men were expected to turn the farm over to their sons or other younger men. Those women who survived childbirth were better able to maintain farm-wife chores even in later years and did not need to pass on their role. In any case, their daughters left home—to work as wives.

In the world of business and industry, men have been able, generation after generation, to see other men coming up behind them, and realize that some younger men inevitably overtake those who are older and more experienced but perhaps worn out, or bored, or less able. It has no doubt always been a psychological blow, but several things mitigated that blow: examples abounded in the persons of other men who were in the same situation or probably would be; past, visible generations had already experienced the same blows; and, crucially, most men had the same opportunities as they started up the ladder—equal access to education and training had generally been available to most men of similar backgrounds.

This was not so for women. Female professionals now over forty have had few examples of women's professional roles in organizations, and almost none of women in supervisory positions. Suddenly older women, some of whom have worked their way up and some of whom are returning as mature people to the work force after a child-rearing hiatus, find themselves subordinate to women who are almost a full generation younger. Nothing in their experience has led them to expect this. For many years they have either been climbing the work ladder, reporting to men or an occasional older woman, or running a mini-corporation in the home where they have acted as chief executive officer and final authority.

What are they to make of this sudden transformation from Somebody to Nobody? From upward job mobility or autonomy, to second (or lower) in command to a younger and perhaps less experienced newcomer?

And what of the newcomer? No problems may appear to exist for her. Today's young executive women became teenagers just as Betty Friedan unleashed her feminine mystique bombshell. Concurrently, other women began to suggest publicly that life could be more than home and family. The Radcliffe Institute (now the Bunting Institute, named after its founder, Mary I. Bunting, an early clear thinker on the possibilities for women and work) solicited its first women for financially supported research of their own choosing in 1960. Radical times in higher education followed, with numerous benefits to girls and young women, who now have access to formerly all-male bastions—from graduate schools like the Harvard Business School down through activities formerly segregated by sex such as Little League and all-male prep schools.

Our interest in this topic sprang from our own professional situations at the time of the research. We are both well educated, career-minded, and in our forties. We have raised children, managed boisterous households, and worked throughout. We have been in charge of departments and been subordinates in other departments. We have worked with and for both men and women, younger and older. We have worked in the corporate sector and in academia. We consider ourselves "successful."

Oddly, we both found ourselves working for much younger women at exactly the same time. We discussed this issue from a personal perspective before investigating it as a research topic. One of us worked for a fifteen-years-younger, overconfident, well-educated woman who was on a very fast track. Many found her manner and style offensive. She was single and spent much of her time talking about her ability to be all things, including sexy and desirable to men.

The other one of us worked for a woman thirteen years younger, also well educated, but with a very different personality and management style. She was confident, happy, caring, and fair. She worked hard at her supervisory skills because she knew she was less experienced in this area. She had a marvelous sense of humor; she could step back and say, "Be patient with me, I'm still learning from you."

Currently, neither of us works for a younger woman.

Of course, our experiences were not unique. As a result of the dual phenomena of highly trained and well-educated young women beginning their careers at managerial levels, and large numbers of older women entering or reentering the work force at subordinate levels, it is common for older women to work for younger ones. Perhaps understandably, this situation has created significant tensions. Sometimes these tensions are simply the result of differences in world views and life-styles, but often there is more than a suggestion of anger and resentment:

> If I had hired a younger woman to work on this project, she would have thought it a privilege and that would have been enough. It was not enough for this woman, and she let me know it.

> I was the new management style, and she was expecting the old style. She just could not work with someone younger because she needed the reinforcement of all the trappings, authoritarian manner and age being the main ones.

> I am amazed by the way she [the younger woman] does not hesitate to bring private matters into public view.

> I knew I was in charge, and I knew my job. The problem was that she [the subordinate] did not know that. It took time for me to win her over.

> I know a cocky young snip whose position has gone to her head. Many women here have been working thirty years or more, and she ought to respect that.

> It is natural that older women who are very good might be resentful of the whippersnapper.

> I read *Passages* with tears streaming down my face wondering who I would be when I was sixty. Now I am at work for a woman expecting her first baby, and I have three teenage sons.

> In the beginning the woman I worked for had more problems with authority than I did. She had to show outsiders that she was in charge. She has grown now and has less need to put on the professional shell.

To tackle this emerging issue we interviewed twenty women, ten defined as "older," by which we meant over forty, and ten as "younger," or under thirty-five. They were about evenly distributed between high-technology firms and not-for-profit firms. Eleven were married; nine either were not now married or had never been. All the married women had children, mostly fewer than three.

In our literature search on women in management and their career paths, and on the psychology of women, we could find nothing that addressed the respective ages of supervisors and supervisees, and no mention of situations in which women supervise women. There is a small body of information and journalism on the experiences of men who work for women—still a pressing issue for some—but the phenomenon of female supervisors outranking older female subordinates has not surfaced.

Interviews were conducted either in person or on the telephone. Most interviews lasted between half an hour and an hour. The small-sample technique afforded us a series of mini case studies, which form the basis for our findings. The questions were open ended and centered around four ideas:

1. Without models, how does each woman play out her work role?

2. Where does the older woman go in career options from where she is?

3. How does the older woman accept the younger woman's knowledge of the working world? Conversely, how does the younger woman manage someone who has lived so much longer, been bumped around more, perhaps led a richer life?

4. Is the older woman looked down on for accepting the subordinate role, or does the younger woman derive status from it? Are both true?

These were our original ideas, and themes recurring over the course of the interviews demonstrated that this initial set of questions was crucial that there were serious management problems at work that specifically applied to women. Authority questions, resentment, occasional denial, fear, anger—all these surfaced in a very short time, and we found some answers to our original queries.

Models and Mentors

Without models, how does each woman play out her part? Sometimes the only model available to both older and younger women is a familiar one from outside the workplace. There is a mother / daughter image in many of these pairings—each viewing the other woman as either a "mother" or a "daughter." Even if a woman's real-life relationship as mother or daughter is good, there may be throwbacks to these private-life roles that play themselves out on the job. Said one older woman, about to accept an offer for a position with a younger woman, "I hope she had a good relationship with her mother." The situation works both ways. As one young manager said, "When I was making a hiring decision, I picked the older woman who expressed a good relationship with her daughter." Others commented as well on the general confusion about how to feel and act.

> Susan, a forty-five-year-old trainee in a financial institution, sits in classes each day with recent college graduates selected through campus recruiting by the bank. She feels lucky to have been selected and knows the bank has made an exception by allowing her into the program, but she goes home each night to her husband and asks him questions about what the women in his office wear and how much of her personal life she ought to be sharing with her peers. There is no other woman in the bank her age whose situation is even remotely similar.

Role models are out there; they can be found. As in groups like Weight Watchers and Parents without Partners, people searching for an opportunity to discuss similar problems can be brought together informally. Personnel departments should be sensitive to this issue and organize focus groups around it. Ruthanne Edwards and Sarah Heller might have been helped by just such a group.

In commenting on the notion of role models, the younger women we interviewed made the following remarks:

> In my company [a small software company] some of the older people banded together because the younger people were threatening.

Upward Mobility

Where does the older woman go from where she is? The problem of where the older woman goes next professionally is very real. At first she is so thrilled to be working again that she does not focus on the mobility factor, but eventually she must ask the question. The younger woman isn't sure where she might move, either, and may feel unsure of how to be a mentor. The older woman may put this problem on the back burner for the moment because she feels she is in a learning position, but both members of the pair will agree that this becomes a big problem eventually.

Often the answer to the question of where the older woman moves in her career (or at least in the particular job situation in which she finds herself) is *nowhere*. But, after all, many jobs are a dead end for both men and women, old and young. Is this really a problem, from a short-range point of view? Again, this issue can be discussed in a group. Since a great deal of research has been done concerning jobs that lead nowhere and there has been much dialogue over the past few years on this topic, it is a rich area to explore, with suggested solutions ranging from enriching one's personal life to changing work environments.

Ellen knows her job will lead nowhere. Her boss is fourteen years younger and has no intention of moving on until her new baby is in school full time. Ellen likes her work but feels locked in for the next six years.

An older woman in our survey, commenting on the lack of a chance to move up, said, "Older women understand that this is part of the game going on and are glad to have the job." But a younger woman who has an older woman reporting to her said: "The older women working for me are not overly interested in learning why things are done. They seem to feel there is no sense in learning new things." Having just gotten in, they find the concept of moving up a remote one. But to a younger woman who never doubted her ability to get in, moving up is an immediate problem. Eventually, of course, the older women we interviewed who had gone back to work several years ago were now facing the upward mobility problem and finding it very real and frustrating.

One strong recommendation from those who raised the issue was to address the mobility problem early on—even in the job interview, if possible. A statement on the topic from the supervisor might be worded as follows:

> I know you're not thinking now about where you might want to go
> in the future from this position, but you will eventually. Right now

you're delighted to have been offered work that is challenging and in your field of interest. But believe me, in a couple of years, when the challenge is no longer there, you'll be saying, "What's next?" Since there really is no place to move up into in this department, or very possibly even within the company, you and I both need to be aware of outside opportunities. We should both keep our eyes open for potential openings for you after you've been here a year or so.

Smart but Not Wise

How does the older woman accept the younger woman's knowledge of the working world? Conversely, how does the younger woman manage someone who has lived so much longer? Knowledge of the working world can become secondary to other concerns. With some exceptions, and with the important factor of their awareness of the issue, older women resented younger female supervisors, who seemed smart but not wise. In some cases this was blatant. Ruthanne and Sarah are obviously struggling with this very question, but so are Audrey and Hilary. At thirty-eight, Audrey knows that Hilary is miles beyond her in business acumen. But when Hilary, twenty-six and in her first real job since graduating with an MBA, panics when she has to give a presentation to a group of vice presidents, Audrey patiently coaches her. Secretly she wishes *she* could give the talk. Years of addressing church groups have made Audrey a polished speaker—and she really knows the content. Such a situation need not yield to bitterness and conflict, however. Rational, productive alterntives *are* available.

One focus group, for example, used an exercise in which women literally traded what they had to offer aloud: "I can give you my editing skills if you will set aside time for the next few weeks to teach me how the budget is put together," said one older subordinate to her boss in the corporate communications department of a high-technology company. Not all knowledge can be neatly transferred, since so much comes from experience; but the point here is that the spirit of collaboration has begun. Ruthanne Edwards could give Sarah her "three quick tips" on dealing with a student who falls apart in a counseling session. Sarah Heller could introduce Ruthanne to an assistant deal in another area of the school who could help her car pool children. The trade is not a big one, but the generosity and concern are obvious.

The personal lives of both women have an impact on their professional relationship. If both are married or both are single, there seem to be fewer problems because each understands the other's problems. If only one in the pair is married, however, there is apt to be envy or jealousy on the part of the unmarried woman, regardless of whether she is older or younger.

Status and Stigma?

Is the older woman looked down on for accepting this subordinate position, or does the younger woman derive status from it? Are both true? For the older woman, there is a definite stigma attached to the pairing. She not only has a woman for a boss but a younger person at that! The older woman acknowledges this problem and wishes it away by saying the situation is only temporary. None of the older women we talked with would be willing to accept the situation forever or even for a long period of time. Why? Because of the discomfort it causes. We are a society geared to working for bosses who are older, bosses who are men. We have an image in our heads of what the boss should look like; beyond being wise and fair, he is silver-haired. He is never a she, and certainly not younger. None of us has been conditioned to the idea that a younger person, perhaps the age of a daughter or son, would ever make decisions about our salary, what tasks we will undertake, and how well those tasks have been performed. Imagine the elves being older than Santa Claus, and you begin to see how ingrained is our mental picture of boss-subordinate relationships.

Martha is delighted to have Sally, an older woman with a doctorate, working for her, even though Martha's own MBA is from a top-ranked school. Martha and Sally are two of the women we interviewed; as with many in our sample, the older woman in the pair had an advanced degree. Sometimes she even "out-degreed" her younger boss. Sally, however, makes a point of explaining to everyone who asks about her new job that she has only taken the position for a year. "I need to pick up some solid marketing background before I move on, she says, "and Martha is the perfect person from whom to get this." Sally has seen the puzzled look on the faces of several co-workers when she tells them about her now job in Martha's department, and she has decided to footnote her announcement with this explanation.

Younger women with whom we spoke made these remarks about the stigma/status issue:

> My secretary (twenty years older) called me "the kid" for a while and seemed to view being there as "playing house." She could not take me seriously.

> You can make trouble for yourself if you believe that older women have nothing to teach you.

> In some ways they are merely tolerant because of their greater experience. They think of ways to work around me gracefully.

> Sometimes there is a lot of envy of young women who were encouraged to go out and get expertise.

Older women had these comments:

> One reason I stalled so long before finally accepting the job was the thought of what I would tell people. I knew there would be raised eyebrows.

> My old boss from another part of the company called me and said, "I understand you're going to work for _____.
> Are you sure that makes sense?" Even after I explained why, he still wondered why I would be willing to do something so foolish.

> When I told a friend I was working for a woman ten years younger than me, he said, "You're going backward in your career, aren't you?"

A number of questions arise concerning the notion of stigma. We did not explore them in our limited look at the issue of the older woman as subordinate.

If the younger woman derives status from supervising an older woman, where does the status come from? Does the stigma create a bad emotional environment between the two employees? What happens if the older woman's job is not temporary, or at least lasts longer than either woman expected? Why does the older woman feel she may have slipped backward in her career when she works for a younger woman? Does the stigma exist because of the position or because of the boss? These questions deserve much more investigation.

The answer to this fourth question, then, is yes, there is a stigma problem for the older woman, and possibly also an increase in status for the younger boss, which is not a problem unless the subordinate feels the stigma quite seriously. Making the arrangement temporary helps lessen the negative effects; when it is possible to acknowledge and announce the temporary nature of the job, the older woman at least tends to feel more comfortable.

Conclusions

It still is not clear to us whether we are talking about a supervision problem, an age problem, or a gender problem. All three are woven into our research and subsequent discussion. There is a phenomenon that does exist when younger professional women supervise older professional women, a relatively new situation that has emerged only in the past five or ten years. It has no counterpart with male professionals and may be short-lived as fewer women take large chunks of time out for child-rearing. It is a situation that may not exist at all in ten years. For historical reasons, therefore, it deserves attention. More important, we can hope to learn something about supervision in general, and we can certainly help those women, both older and younger, who for the next ten or twenty years will find themselves caught in this phenomenon. The realities of the educational system, combined with some affirmative action support and general change in social mores, will permit more freedom to women for at least another generation to enter the marketplace better trained than the women they supervise. Since these ideas seem to be typical of the thoughts and reactions of older women, organizational behavior problems exist that must be addressed.

First, organizations must be willing to identify and deal with the issue, as they rececently have in instances of sexual harassment. For women already working, it may be enough that the personnel representative knows a situation exists and is willing to watch it or to be sure both sides can agree. Focus groups have been suggested in the chapter as a good arena for sharing concerns.

Techniques for exploring and resolving the issue can come out of conflict-resolution activities that already exist in the workplace. Ultimately, the employer wants to increase productivity and to lower turnover. If this growing segment of the work force can end its hidden conflict, another chapter will be written in the improvement of working conditions for women and for all workers.

8

Separate Strengths: How Men and Women Manage Conflict and Competition

Bonnie R. Kasten

I recently attended a reunion of charter members of a professional women's organization started in the early 1970s. We convened to compare notes and tell business war stories. In 1976 forty women founded this organization, thirty-six of them female corporate executives. Today only fifteen are employed by corporations, most in positions similar to those they held ten years ago. More significantly, twenty-one former corporate loyalists are now working outside of corporate America, most running their own successful businesses.

On another occasion, I had the opportunity to interview senior men and women from a high-tech multinational company. The concern being addressed was how to develop middle-management women for senior executive positions. One by one, women made comments about plans to leave because their career paths didn't match senior management's plans for them. These situations highlight what has become crystal clear: women are leaving many male-dominated organizations at alarming rates.

Company executives are confused. They expend large sums of money and resources to recruit females; the women are brought along to upper-middle-management positions—and then they leave. The corporation, of course, blames the women: "She just isn't committed. She isn't loyal. She wasn't really serious about a career anyway."

Thirty-seven-year-old Jill heard this criticism when she left a large energy company to start her own business. On her last day with the company, her boss's final comment was, "I really went out on a limb for you and this is how you repay me!" A senior vice-president confronted her in the company cafeteria with this parting shot: "We gave you a good title; we gave you a lot of money; but you girls just aren't ready to play by the rules. Loyalty is what counts, and you just don't have it."

The numbers of women in corporate America stay constant, but those women who hit the so-called glass ceiling (where they can see the executive boardroom, but can't get in) are leaving, and new women are coming in at the bottom. The conclusion of a number of studies is that women are kept out of senior management positions simply because senior-level men are less comfortable with women than with their male counterparts. It's a question of fit.

The career ladder for women seems, therefore, to stop at the middle-management level. If you watch the career progression of men and women, you can almost see two ladders, one for women and one for men—and the women's ladder has invisible rungs.

Imagine yourself climbing a ladder and inadvertently missing a step. You're afraid you'll fall, and you're probably embarrassed. Corporate women often step out for the next career rung only to find it missing. Many are choosing instead to get off the ladder.

Are men and women colluding in keeping the rungs invisible? Does competitiveness distort women's perceptions and blind men to the gaping hole in the ladder for women? Are fit and comfort between men and women at senior management levels tied to different rules for fighting and competing? After talks with hundreds of frustrated career women and many confused men, it is becoming apparent that both women and men must learn to manage conflict appropriately. They need to develop better mechanisms for handling competition. If they can do this, the likelihood of men and women jointly occupying executive positions will increase. Women will no longer want to leave corporations just as they are beginning to flex their organizational muscle.

Conflict and *competition* are difficult concepts to define. People ascribe different meaning to these emotionally loaded words. We need some common framework to understand these concepts.

Conflict is natural. Animals are aroused into a fight-or-flight pattern when they experience conflict. The natural human and animal reaction is to stand up and fight or to run away. Now superimpose male and female social conditioning on a conflict situation. Men are socialized to confront, to "stand up and take it like a man." Women are taught that "it's not ladylike to fight." What are women to do when they experience workplace conflict? In a competitive business environment they need a more appropriate response than to flee or remain silent.

The second concept is more subtle. Male-to-male competition has prescribed roles. Competition between men and women, however, is confused by sexual overtones. Traditionally, being a man meant you fought battles over territories and principles; women were the reward. When women and men compete, issues of physical force and dominance emerge: "Don't hurt the little woman." It's generally accepted that men can initiate seductive behavior, whether in the boardroom or the bar. Women, however, must not initiate openly, or they are labeled loose or unprofessional. These and other traditional rules of sexual competition are still very much alive in corporate America. Although things are changing, these dynamics still exist; they are simply more subtle or disguised. They are an inappropriate foundation for business transactions because they confuse competition with sexual dominance; they reinforce competition according to different gender-prescribed ground rules.

Unhealthful conflict in the workplace robs men and women of dignity, not to mention productivity. It asks both men and women to fit gender-specific roles. It severely limits their repertoire for interaction. As men and women, we have, different beliefs and assumptions from which we operate. We need to take the best that each has to offer and thereby expand our opportunities for interaction so we can better manage conflict. We can maintain our dignity by negotiating constructively. Managing conflict through negotiation means being involved in healthful competition. In such competitive environment, conflict is acknowledged and addressed, not ignored.

Conflict as a Natural Interest

It is useful to consider what we're talking about here in terms of energy forces. The way we choose to use our human energy determines our impact on others. Energy masses can be turbulent or calm, in motion or stagnant. In interactions, we experience one another through an energy filter: he's intense, she's lively, he's laid back, she's quiet. In these terms, we decide if we like or dislike someone based on his or her energy.

Frequently, energy is used positively. For instance, sexual attraction between men and women often creates stimulating, sparking energy. Meetings or conferences attended by both men and women actually feel different from all-male or all-female meetings. It is not uncommon for an all-male meeting to be described as dull and lifeless. When men and women meet together, however, sessions often lighten up, and energy is more buoyant. On the other hand, sexual energy can become destructive when competitive behavior focuses on win-lose outcomes, and when aggressive energy is used to attack or defend.

The concept of positive and negative uses of human energy is not new. Psychoanalysts since Freud have described human behavior in terms of energy. Management training programs, especially in negotiating, use the concept of energy flow as a useful teaching tool.[1]

For example, both men and women, especially in corporate settings, highly value the use of *push energy*. That is the kind of energy used to convince others of one's ideas or to make demands and stick up for one's own position. It's energy that pushes your thoughts onto others. When men use push energy, they are exhibiting characteristics that are traditionally gender-appropriate. Men are held to be logical, forceful, quick to defend, confident, and assertive. Push energy is expected and comfortable for men.

When women use push energy, however, they are frequently misread. Men label women who use push energy as bitchy or aggressive. Women sometimes label other women as catty, masculine, or just basically tough and mean. It's uncharacteristic for women to stand firm, say what they want, and compete straightforwardly. When asked why certain women in one company succeeded, other women said that only those masculine women who looked and tried to act like men got ahead, and "we don't want to be like them and lose our ability to be and act like women." The old model for success for women executives has been a variation on the *My Fair Lady* theme: "Why can't a woman be more like a man?"

Women are, however, heavily reinforced when they use *pull energy*. Pull energy is the kind of energy you use to draw others toward you, or to get them to feel "pulled," or kindly disposed, toward you. It's the kind of energy you use to make the other person feel attended to. Like a baby's open arms, it encourages you to come closer. Stereotypically, women are the service providers, the nurturers, the listeners, the thoughtful ones. Men often label pull energy as weak and soft. It is not manly to use pull energy; in fact, it is often described as feminine. Thus stereotyping by gender begins at a level as basic as how we use our human energy.

All animals instinctively fight. They fight over territory, over issues of control and dominance, and over scarce resources. Conflict springs from the drive to protect oneself and one's own from harm; it is a natural part of the life process. But whereas animals fight without thinking, we humans have an added dimension. We have a basic drive to control our destiny, even to the point of wanting to be immortal. Everyone wants to be a hero or heroine, to be unique and stand apart, to live out his or her own images and fantasies.

We experience conflict when we come up against others who also are driven by these same basic drives. Most of us give a large percentage of our lives to our work and our families, so the two arenas where drives are most reinforced are in our work settings and in our homes. Male-dominated corporations are the personification of the drive to acquire resources.

The drive to control one's own destiny has been played out in a predictable way—men have controlled the boardroom, and women have controlled the bedroom. The problem is this: control and power are shifting within both organizations and families. Women, by their numbers alone, are influencing corporate decisions. Men are asking for and taking more responsibility for domestic decisons. A new kind of independence is growing, whereby women make independent business decisions and men make independent domestic decisions. As this societal transformation occurs, changing the previous notions of control and power, major, deep-seated, fundamental conflicts about values and beliefs emerge and are acted on, most of them in unconscious ways.

Millenia of Gender-Typed Conditioning

From childhood on, women are told they can get what they want by being dependent on others. To get what they want, they are socialized to give—give of their bodies, give of their good deeds, and take care of others in order to get love. To identify what they want as their due and ask for it openly is foreign to them. What a woman wants must be granted by others, not negotiated from an equal position. A woman's wants are not equal, the argument goes, because she is not equal. If she is not equal, then what she wants can't be worth as much.[2]

Men, on the other hand, are taught to be independent: they feel they have a right to ask for what they want. Men take equality with other men for granted. That is, the fight for position with other men begins from an equal starting point in life. Women traditionally are seen as great because of their service to others, whereas men earn greatness by their deeds. Men fight for their place in destiny; women gain immortality through the men with whom they associate.

Moral development patterns for boys and girls are different. According to recent research, boys, when confronted with a moral conflict, tend to focus on individual choice.[3] They solve the problem by deciding what's right. Girls, confronted with the same moral conflict, tend to see the problem as one of communication—in other words, one of relationship. Thus our notions of conflict and competition are deeply rooted in an incredible morass of values and beliefs based on gender differentiation or traditional sex-role behavior.

One young women sleeps with her boss. Another woman uses the bedroom to close a deal or keep a client. A male boss propositions his secretary. In corporation after corporation, men and women use sex as a way of handling competition. If you want to get ahead, and you're a woman, it is very likely that some time in your corporate career you'll be offered the proverbial carrot if you agree to sleep with someone. One of the few equalizers of power in the corporate world of haves and have-nots is sex. Both men and women believe that women sleep their way up the corporate ladder. Sexual attraction and sexual harassment are controversial corporate topics. The name of the game is power; and the rules of the game were formed, it seems, on the school playground through sex-role conditioning.

If you observe boys and girls playing in schoolyards, you'll see the following pattern. Boys yell to one another: "Beat you to the gym!" or "Bet your Dad isn't as important as mine." Boys compete with other boys in games, especially in bouts of physical exhibitionism. Boys and men learn to compete early on for prizes—better cars, better jobs, more money. They learn to jockey for position to win—to win for the sake of winning. All competitive tactics seem to lead to that end. Boys usually don't compete with girls because they won't earn the same respect if they beat a girl as they will if they beat a boy: "You let her beat you. What are you, a sissy?!"

Men compete with other men for women. A male colleague and I were on a balcony, and we observed the following scene unfold beneath us. Fifteen men and one woman were gathered on a law at dusk, following a training session. The drinks were flowing, and the chatter was punctuated with spontaneous chuckles. We began to notice that the group had a predictable movement to it. It was as if the woman were a magnet and the men were iron filings. As she moved, some men approached and others backed off. The kaleidoscope below us changed as she stepped from place to place. Men not immediately attending to her would bunch on the perimeter and cast sidelong glances in her direction. This same scene, where one woman is an object and both men and women unconsciously are pressured to behave in prescribed ways, can be seen over and over again in corporate settings.

Girls on the playground cluster in tight groups to discuss boys. They watch what the boys do, describe how they feel about boys, and discuss what the boys like and don't like. They calculate how best to get a boy's attention and coaxing each other to deliver messages to particular boys. Girls and then women have been socialized to compete with one another for men's attention. Women will even do one another in, often using subtle, nonconfrontational methods. When it comes to defending her man—be he boss, lover, colleague, or attractive guy down the hall—a woman stereotypically will fight whatever the cost.

As women move up the corporate ladder, they become greater threats to males. The competition heightens. When a woman is young and at a low level, she can be "mentored"—that is, shown kindness and looked after and given pats on the head. Men do not feel particularly threatened by her. As women enter upper management positions, however, they quickly become more visible and more threatening. The competition become sharper. As one forty-two-year-old male senior executive commented when told the person consulting to the executive team would be a woman: "Bright women are the most dangerous kind." A woman, in order to be successful, has to reject a lifetime of the following beliefs and values:

I don't really have legitimate rights.

Winning produces guilt.

The helping role is truly the legitimate one.

Relationships are more important than getting what I want (or winning, or knowing that what I want will sacrifice a relationship).

When a woman approaches the glass ceiling and can't rely on the traditional roles of nurturer/supporter—or, in some cases, plaything—she may find herself unarmed at a critical juncture in her corporate career. Because she is trying to challenge the norms, she is often unwilling to confuse her sexual and professional lives.

Some women learn, however, to use their gender to disarm the conflict. This is often seen as a professional version of so-called feminine wiles. She learns not to provoke. She raises sticky issues in private; she smiles rather than confronts. Men tease her, and she flirts back but doesn't deliver. She constantly watches for male come-ons and monitors her own as well. Even in a corporate power context, it's her responsibility to manage this kind of social and sexual tension. In legitimate corporate conflicts over roles, responsibilities, or resources, women will more often read nonverbal cues—that is, they will "psych out" the male opposition. A typical tactic for a woman to take is to try to figure out the men and actually take her cues from the men with whom she is competing. Reading the competitive environment usually means reading men.

A colleague of mine describes his reaction to working with women colleagues this way: "When I'm negotiating and there's a woman in the discussion, it opens up competition between the men. I'm aware of my presence as a male; I'm more conscious of being a male, and I then need to prove my maleness. This often takes the competition into unhealthy one-ups*man*ship."

Typically, men's behavior in conflict with other men is to be aggressive. When men are in competitive situations with women, however, seduction is often added to the list. "If I can get a saleswoman to stop talking shop and flirt with me, I've changed the balance of power in this situation," said this colleague. When I ask men and women to describe what they value in how men handle conflict, the responses overwhelmingly sound like, "He takes the other on," or "He goes all out to win," or "He doesn't give in."

When men and women describe what they value in how women handle conflict, the responses sound more like, "She's willing to give a little," or "She doesn't get upset," or "She listens to others' opinions." Men are valued for competing. Women are valued for being receptive—for accommodating, giving in, or smoothing over conflict.

Women know that these expected behaviors won't work any more. Men have been slower in acknowledging their role in gender conflict; but both men and women are experiencing different tensions, frustration, and confusion about how to handle each other. For instance, neither men nor women have to spend as much time thinking about how to interact with same-sex colleagues. Men who are used to swearing, however, will hesitate with women present. Women will have to decide how to respond when a sexist joke is told in a group of men. More conscious decisions must be made, and this requires a different kind of energy. Energy must be shifted from moving *against* to moving *with*. Men and women need to collaborate on a new joint venture—a venture that will reinforce attitude and behavior style shifts.

Negotiating from Equality

The word *collaboration* is the key. Until both men and women learn a new behavior pattern for competing—that is, a pattern that creates fair and not coercive competition—the issues of power and winning will continue to be fought on gender battlegrounds.

There are many ways of describing behaviors when one is in a conflict situation. You can compete like a hawk or approach the situation like a dove—or an ostrich, or a weasel. The range of competitive behavior is wide. Collaboration, however, is a mind-set. The attitude with which you approach a conflict determines your behavior pattern. Try entering a discussion mad as a March hare, but behaving lovingly and supportively, or try entering a situation as excited as a child at a circus and behaving somberly and quietly. Your mind-set shows through!

Collaboration, then, is the mind-set needed to resolve conflict. However, the skills needed to collaborate and thereby resolve conflict in corporations are more often associated with negotiating. Negotiation is a process that acknowledges that people have vested interests—that in organizations where people have diverse roles and functions, legitimate differences are inherent and are to be respected. For instance, when male and female supervisors discuss which work group is going to get additional help, both are short-handed and only one position is allocated, the optimum negotiated agreement would be for both to get partial use of the additional help. If one wins at the the expense of the other, the two will find future negotiations far more difficult.

At budget time, directors often need to negotiate for their own department because of conflicting departmental goals. If one's mind-set is to get all you can regardless of the others, the likelihood of peer disapproval can prove problematic. If, however, all parties look for creative ways to meet each other's needs, the departments run more smoothly. Both sides have shown respect for the interests and needs of the other. Nothing goes farther in corporate diplomacy than attending to the interests of competitors.

Management negotiating that maintains and builds relationships is the ideal; people need to work toward agreement in open, straightforward ways. People will, of course, try to meet their own needs. At the same time they must work to preserve the dignity of others.

This kind of negotiating is based on a special set of skills. Some of these skills come naturally to women, some more easily to men.

Over the last ten years, I've taught more than three thousand men and women complex influence and negotiation skills. I've noticed that distinct behavior patterns emerge in women and in men. All men and women certainly don't exhibit these behaviors. the tendency, however, is for women to exhibit the following types of successful negotiation behavior:

They listen attentively and often clarify the other's position.

They use logic to support their ideas.

The comment on areas of agreement.

They avoid provoking the other person.

Men tend more often to exhibit the following, also appropriate behavior:

They make firm proposals and demands.

They make few concessions and hold their positions.

They use time as their ally.

They bargain to get what they want.

All these behaviors are necessary to negotiate successfully. Negotiation research indicates clearly that people who reach successful, lasting agreements use all eight of the foregoing behaviors. If men and women would learn to develop the other sex's strengths, then each gender would have a full complement of skills. Women will be better negotiators and conflict managers when they overcome their fear of asking for what they want; men will be better negotiators when they learn to listen—*really* listen—to different voices.

> Men and women may speak different languages that they assume are the same, using similar words to encode disparate experiences of self and social relationships. Because these languages share an overlapping moral vocabulary, they contain a propensity for systematic mistranslation, creating misunderstandings which impede communication and limit the potential for cooperation and care in relationships.[4]

Both men and women must overcome lifetimes of gender-biased social development in order to develop the negotiation strengths of the other sex. Only when face-to-face confrontation is managed straightforwardly will men and women be able to give up their gender battles and learn new power rules.

Power has always been and continues to be the real issue at stake, both in games of competition and in arenas of conflict. Again, learning that power is not a zero-sum game (that is, if one has power another can't) is an important lesson for both men and women. Power does not have to be a limited resource. Although power is often associated with position and authority, one is far more influential using commitment and not control to motivate others. Even the lowest person on the organizational totem pole has power if he or she can get others to work in concert with him or her.

Power is a funny thing—it's primarily a matter of perception. If you have power but I don't think so, then you don't really have it. If you don't really have power but I think you do, then you do. If you have power in a negotiation, you have the ability to affect favorably someone else's position. One can argue that your power depends on someone else's perception of your strength; it is what they *think* you have that matters, not what you actually have.

Women and men have different perceptions of the source of their negotiating power. In the past, gender, sexual norms, and physical force have determined rules for power. When we strip away these traditional rules for balancing the power, the following three categories serve us well as foundations for establishing new rules for balancing power between men and women.[5]

1. *The power of skill and knowledge.* In a competitive environment, research shows that a skilled negotiator will be better at influencing the decisions of others than will an unskilled negotiator.[6] Being skilled at negotiating means having a process or road map to follow, having the ability to choose and use the appropriate behavior at the right time in the negotiation, and using the knowledge of the situation and one's skills in such a way as to bring about a successful and fair agreement. The skilled negotiator determines the other's personal concerns, values, and hopes; he or she assesses the other's underlying interests. Women are particularly skilled at doing this. What was formerly called *intuition* is now appropriately labeled *perceptual skill*, which many women develop early in life. Women have learned to notice subtle distinctions in the other person's voice, position, words, and so on.

Knowledge of background facts, social and legal implications, and history are all of great advantage to skilled negotiators. Both men and women have the capacity to do the kind of research necessary and marshal the appropriate facts to arm them in organizational conflict. Having facts, not inferences, at hand makes it easier for a woman not to be dismissed.

2. *The power of a good relationship.* Your power in a negotiation depends on whether or not the other side can trust you. Your reputation precedes you in an organizational confrontation. If you have a reputation for being candid, for acting with integrity, for being concerned about the relationship, your power increases. Trust begets trust. If you have a reputation for lecturing or treating others in a condescending manner, you will be treated with suspicion. If you've misrepresented information, your ability to get others to listen to you is severely diminished. It's up to you not to slip. Trust is as delicate as a gossamer thread; once broken, it is very difficult to mend.

3. *The power of clean communication.* Good negotiating relationships also stem from clean communication. Clean communicating means a willingness to permit give and take. Each side acknowledges the dignity of the other. Both men and women need to take a fresh look at communicating from a give-and-take position. A female senior executive once said: "They [the men] don't even see me, let alone hear me. I have to work extremely hard just to be heard." If men and women are going to find a way to communicate, men will have to see women as executives first and women second. In the 1980s we have a gender-reference for the word *executive* and we have a different gender-reference for the word *secretary*. The gender-reference implies very different organizational power bases. Men and women must negotiate in a way that benefits the organization; they both need to learn to assess the power balance on the basis of how the parties communicate the positions they truly hold, not of what they stereotypically represent. Powerful women are threatening to men. Often, when women are first invited to a corporate meeting, the male-to-male questioning begins, "What's she look like?" or "What—a woman!." Clean communication will result if the men ask business-related questions instead: "What's her expertise?" "What role will she play?" Then we'll see both men and women listening and hearing true messages.

Who's Got the Competitive Edge?

What will happen to competition among men and women as the rules change? One definition of competition is vying with others for profit, prize, position, or the necessities of life. If both men and women can educate each other through mutually open communication about values, assumptions, fears, and hopes, then the basis for a competitive environment that has collaboration as a goal will emerge. Men need to stop thinking in zero-sum ways; women need to identify what they want, ask for it, and not wilt if attacked.

Negotiation skills can be learned so that all people have basic tools to start from. Healthy competition will be encouraged and differences will be examined as men and women try to reach mutually equitable agreements. Healthy competition will equal healthy conflict. The energy now expended on unhealthy conflict and competition will be shifted to energy expended on resolution and building relationships. Women will be able to continue up the corporate ladder, for the rungs will no longer be invisible. Men and women will have learned to manage conflict so that everyone wins. And the result will be increased and aligned productivity.

Notes

1. David Berlew, Alex Moore, and Roger Harrison, *Positive Negotiation Trainer Manual* (Plymouth, Mass.: Powder Horn Press, 1984).
2. Jean Baker Miller, *Toward a New Psychology of Women* (Boston, Mass.: Beacon Press, 1976).
3. Carol Gilligan, *In a Different Voice* (Cambridge, Mass.: Harvard University Press, 1982).
4. Gilligan, *Different Voice*, p. 173.
5. R. Fisher, *Negotiating Power* (Beverly Hills, Calif.: Sage Publications, 1983).
6. Berlew, *Positive Negotiation Trainer Manual.*

References

Becker, E. 1973. *The Denial of Death*. New York: The Free Press.
Braker, S. 1984. "Why Women Aren't Getting to the Top." *Fortune*, April 16.
Hofstede, G. 1980. *Culture's Consequences*. Beverly Hills, Calif.: Sage.
Kanter, R.M. 1977. *Men and Women of the Corporation*. New York, Basic Books.

9

Our Game, Your Rules: Developing Effective Negotiating Approaches

Leonard Greenhalgh
Roderick W. Gilkey

Consider the following scenario: A female manager is having a discussion with a male counterpart. They are trying to reach agreement on some issue in dispute. The woman takes a flexible, friendly stance; the man is argumentative and holds firmly to his position. When they have made little progress toward agreement after some time, the woman makes concessions, telling the man she will give in on this issue and he can make it up to her next time. Some time after the negotiation is over, she learns that he did not disclose all the information he must have had, and that he even made some claims that subsequently proved to be untrue. But she gave him the benefit of the doubt on both these points; she figured he must have become a little confused while arguing for his position.

A couple of weeks later, they meet again to try to reach agreement on another issue in dispute. The woman politely reminds the man that she was generous on the last issue and therefore it is *his* turn to show some flexibility. He dismisses this reminder out of hand and proceeds to take a firm stand on the current issue. The woman, feeling angry and betrayed, now blames herself for being too unassertive.

The scenario is a familiar one. Assertiveness training, however, is not the answer to this woman's problem. Her poor short-term per-

The authors gratefully acknowledge the contribution of Susan M. Pufahl and Lucy Axtell to the development of this chapter.

formance in this negotiation will show little improvement if all she learns are firmer ways of expressing herself. Instead, she needs to understand that there tends to be a fundamental difference in the way men and women view such interactions.

Women in organizations need to understand this difference because the ability to negotiate is a crucial skill in male-dominated organizational life. In theory, business decisions are rational conclusions drawn when problems are considered in the abstract. In practice, however, most significant decisions in organizations emerge from a process of negotiation; that is, reaching the decision involves reconciling the conflicting interests of the people who have some say in the matter. Making an organizational decision that is acceptable and can be implemented may require negotiating with a host of people—peers, subordinates, superiors, people in staff or control roles, customers, suppliers, regulators, news media representatives, perhaps even family members and others who may be indirectly affected by the decision. Most of the time, these people are not conscious of the fact that they are negotiating. Nevertheless, negotiation is such a basic process in organizations that development of people's negotiating skills is as important as any other area of professional development.

During the past seven years of teaching negotiating skills to managers, executives, and MBAs in training for careers in organizations, we sensed a difference in the way men and women approach negotiation. We analyzed videotapes of simulated negotiation and found some of the differences reported in the popular press. For example, we saw that women are more likely to use powerless speech: instead of saying, "Your price is too high based on what your competitors are charging," they tend to say something like, "I don't suppose you'd consider a slightly lower price." Such hesitant, unassuming ways of making a point invite an uncooperative response if the other person is looking for a short-term gain. Women tended to demand less and concede more.

We weren't satisfied, however, that we really understood the nature and full implications of this difference in approach. We studied the relevant literature in social, personality, and developmental psychology, and saw a link between early developmental experiences, adult personality, and the negotiating behavior of young professionals. We then conducted a study to investigate the relationships we expected to find. As a result, we now have a better-informed idea of how to train men and women to reach agreements.

In this chapter, we will talk about what we have learned from our research and how this information is useful in developing women's skills as negotiators.

Backgrounds

One of the most important factors affecting your approach to negotiation is your time perspective. If you view a negotiation as a single event, you will tend to focus on your immediate gain and probably will not make sacrifices in order to preserve and improve your relationship with the other person. This is known as an *episodic orientation:* you see the negotiation as a single episode whereby the history and future of your relationship with the other person are largely irrelevant. The contrasting time perspective is known as a *continuous orientation.* With such a perspective, you pay attention to the long-term relationship between you and the other person. The present negotiation is one event in a stream of interactions. Therefore, the history and future of the relationship are important—perhaps more important than immediate gain. Thus it is natural to expect that differences in time perspective will lead to differences in negotiating behavior. An episodic orientation should be associated with a competitive approach ("I need to come out ahead in this deal, and it's going to be at your expense"), whereas a continuous orientation should be associated with a more cooperative approach ("Let's find a way to meet both our needs").

Negotiators' different personalities are likely to affect whether they tend to perceive a bargaining situation as more episodic or more continuous. In particular, such differences in time perspective seem to result from a more fundamental difference in men's and women's orientations toward interpersonal relationships. This difference has been noted in a number of studies that have concluded that women tend to be concerned with their need to get along with others, cooperativeness, and fairness to both parties; men, by contrast, are concerned with their own interests, competing, and avoiding being controlled or dominated by others.[1]

One researcher attributes these contrasting orientations to differences in early developmental experiences.[2] Females develop their sex-role identity from an interaction *with* the mother that emphasizes interdependence, whereas males establish their sex-role identity through separation and individuation *from* their mothers. These differing experiences produce fundamental sex differences later in life that lead women to define themselves *in relation* to others and men *in contrast* to others.

A related factor is the difference in the way boys and girls approach games. Boys are brought up to play competitive games, in which the objective is to beat the opponent. It is acceptable to gloat about victory and deride the loser. Girls play games that focus less on winning and losing. In fact, if their games are progressing in such a way that someone is going to feel bad, girls are likely to stop the game or change the rules: girls don't sacrifice relationships in order to win games.

Carol Gilligan, in her now-classic book *In a Different Voice*, examines the consequences of such basic differences when those individuals become older children. She notes that the greater emphasis on interdependence and mutuality in women's development accounts for the difference between the sexes in their perspective on moral dilemmas: women tend to emphasize their long-term responsibilities and men their immediate rights.

Gilligan cites as an example the case of two eleven-year-old children, a boy and a girl, who respond to questions about a moral dilemma. The boy, Jake, uses deductive logic to deal with what he sees as a conflict over rights and principles among three people, and he describes the solution that would quickly resolve the issues. The response of the girl, Amy, seems less clear and more equivocal. It is tempting to view Amy's response as being logically inferior to and less morally mature than Jake's, but on closer examination it becomes clear that she is viewing the conflict in very different terms. For her, the problem is one of trying to resolve a human-relations issue through ongoing personal communication. Jake, by contrast, views it as a conflict over rights that can be resolved through a morally informed legal system (the set of rules by which the "game" is played). Amy's response is actually based on a relatively sophisticated analysis of interpersonal dynamics. Her response calls for an ongoing series of interactions concerned more with preserving the relationships between conflicting parties than with deciding the parties' rights in the immediate situation.

Support for Gilligan's point of view can be found in studies that investigate the motivation of individuals to determine how they relate to other people. For example, some researchers have found a difference between boys and girls in the kinds of achievement toward which they aspire. Boys primarily strive to achieve success and therefore are more task-oriented; girls strive primarily to achieve praise and therefore are more relationship-oriented. Other studies have shown a tendency for males to be more competitive and women more cooperative in their interpersonal interactions.[3] Still other studies have examined whether males and females want different things from their jobs.[4] Those studies examine the view that women tend to be more concerned with interpersonal relationships in the work environment, whereas men appear to be more concerned with such factors as the opportunity for advancement (winning) and greater responsibility and influence (dominance).

One difficulty in conducting these studies is that women react to the experimental situation itself. A group of studies suggests that females appear to be more sensitive than males to a number of interpersonal cues that can influence their responses to the experiments. Such cues include the sex of the experimenter, whether communication is controlled or free in the experiment, and whether fairness issues are involved in the conflict.[5] These factors tend to affect women more than men and may indeed explain why research findings have been inconsistent.

Thus some of the traits that tend to characterize women make it difficult for researchers to identify male-female differences accurately.

Taken as a whole, the diverse studies of gender differences show some general tendencies but are inconsistent in their specific conclusions. The inconsistencies are understandable when one takes into account that the behavior of adult negotiators is a function not only of biological sex but also of the effects of developmental experiences. The different childhood socialization experiences of males and females can result in different sex-role orientations, ranging from strongly masculine to strongly feminine. A strongly masculine person is concerned with power and prefers to dominate others rather than be dominated by them; a strongly feminine person is less concerned with dominance and more concerned with nurturance. Masculinity-feminity, however, does not correspond exactly to biological sex. Some boys are raised to have predominantly feminine orientations, and some girls are raised to have predominantly masculine orientations. All people fall on a continuum between these two extremes. Because sex role is expected to have greater effect on negotiating behavior, sex role rather than biological sex is used in the research reported here and in the discussion that follows.

The Study

Having come this far in researching the literature, we were confident that there were masculine-feminine differences in negotiating approaches. As social scientists, however, we realized that our past observations could simply be hunches, that the studies we had read reported some inconsistencies, and that no one had yet directly studied masculine-feminine differences of adult negotiators. The burden of proof was on us to show that such differences really exist.

We decided to study masculine-feminine differences in a controlled, laboratory setting. Instead of observing everyday negotiations, we simulated the situations under controlled conditions and had young professionals role-play the negotiations. There was enough flexibility in the role instructions to allow masculine-feminine differences to emerge as expected. The use of a laboratory study had two advantages over observing naturally occurring negotiations: First, it allowed us to eliminate most extraneous factors that could contaminate the results; second, it would allow other researchers to replicate our study, thereby adding to its scientific value. (A description of the study can be found at the end of this chapter.)

The results of the study proved consistent with what we had hypothesized. Several differences between masculine and feminine negotiators emerged and are summarized in table 9–1. The most basic finding was that feminine negotiators tend to visualize the long-term relationship between the people involved when they think about negotiations. Their masculine counterparts tend to visualize a sporting event in which the other person is an opponent who has to be beaten.

Table 9–1
*Summary of the Different Tendencies of
Masculine and Feminine Negotiators*

Masculine Tendencies	Feminine Tendencies
Visualize a one-shot deal	Visualize the present transaction as one event in a long-term relationship.
Seek a sports-type victory	Seek mutual gain
Emphasize rules-of-the-game, precedents, and power positions	Emphasize fairness
Explain logic of their position	Inquire about other's needs and make personal appeals
Conceal or misrepresent their own needs	Be up front about their own needs
Speak in a dominating or controlling manner	Use "powerless" speech
Be intransigent about their position, perhaps trying to conceal their rigid stance	Be willing to compromise
Interrupt and deceive the other party	Avoid tactics that might jeopardize the long-term relationship

Consistent with this basic difference in orientation, feminine negotiators were likely to be more emphathic: that is, they had a natural tendency to try to see the situation from the other person's point of view. This put them in a position to meet mutual needs, which is an ideal outcome of negotiations when there is an ongoing relationship. Furthermore, in the absence of an urgency to "win," feminine negotiators sought fairness and were willing to compromise to achieve a fair outcome.

Finally, the feminine negotiators' concern with the long-term relationship seems to lead them to avoid using tactics that might jeopardize that relationship. Thus we found that feminine negotiators were less likely to deceive the other person. Ironically, the stereotypical view of women's and men's relative trustworthiness is just the opposite. When social psychologists ask people whether women or men are more likely to use underhanded tactics, most people choose women as the less trustworthy. Our research shows that, in fact, women are likely to be more trustworthy than men.

Implications for Negotiation Research

The time horizon makes a big difference in how a person approaches a negotiation. If the person visualizes a one-shot deal, any tactic that will produce an advantage is considered because there is no need to worry about future consequences. If, on the other hand, the person's focus is on the longer-term relationship, then immediate gain is less important than maintaining good will.

Two things determine whether a negotiator takes an episodic or a continuous orientation toward a particular transaction. The first is the objective situation: some transactions *are* one-shot deals in which the negotiators have never interacted beforehand and will probably never deal with each other again. Examples of such transactions include buying an item in a bazaar in a foreign country, or selling an automobile through a newspaper advertisement. The second determinant is the negotiator's personality, which may create *tendencies* to perceive the time horizon to be long-term or short-term, regardless of what the objective situation really calls for. We have seen that a person's sex-role orientation, arising from developmental experiences, has such an effect.

The results of this research help explain some of the inconsistencies in the literature on sex differences in interpersonal relations. In many studies, sex is defined in terms of biological gender; but that approach neglects the results of developmental experiences, which vary widely among individuals. If we are confident that sex-role orientation accurately measures the masculine-feminine perspective, it makes more sense to use this dimension rather than biological sex in our research.

This knowledge of masculine-feminine differences in negotiation approaches helps us understand the scenario we presented at the beginning of this chapter. The woman was willing to make concessions in the short term because she visualized a long-term relationship, in which present concessions would be reciprocated in the future. Her male counterpart had no such perspective. He was visualizing a one-shot deal in which the objective was to beat the other party. Because he saw the interaction as a game, any tactics were permissible—including withholding information and outright deception—as long as they did not violate the explicit rules of the game. The future was irrelevant once the game was over, and a victory in a past game did not obligate the man to try less hard in the next. Had the female negotiator realized that the man was approaching the interaction from this perspective, she could have imposed some rules on the game, or convinced the man not to think of it as a game and done a better job of emphasizing the long-term relationship between them.

Implications for Development of Negotiating Skill

Differences in socialization are among the many factors that explain personality differences among negotiators. There is no one best way to negotiate that is suitable for all personalities; rather, each person must develop an approach that capitalizes on unique strengths and compensates for weaknesses. Thus the development of individuals' negotiating approaches must be a highly individualized process that ideally begins with personality assessment.

Personality assessment, however, is not a process that can be taken lightly. The adage that "a little knowledge is a dangerous thing" can be particularly true in the case of understanding one's psychological makeup. Thus the personality-assessment phase of our approach to training negotiators is a comprehensive process, involving standardized self-report personality measures, projective tests, psychological histories, observation of negotiating behavior, and an in-depth interview conducted by a clinical psychologist. Only when we have a good understanding of the individual do we feed back the insights thus gained to the person to improve his or her self-understanding. This process also sensitizes the person both to improve his or her self-understanding and to start thinking about how others may be different, so that negotiating tactics can be somewhat tailored to the type of individual being dealt with. This aspect of our program for developing negotiators is very effective, but we caution individuals who may be undertaking their own self-development, as well as those seeking to develop others, to be sure that properly qualified people are involved in the assessment and that the analysis is comprehensive enough so that it does more good than harm.

Our next step is to help people valuate their effectiveness as negotiators, given their uniqueness as individuals. The best way to do this is to help people become good self-critics. They learn to assess the effectiveness of their negotiating approaches by analyzing a videotape of their own negotiation performance. We have found that people tend to downplay their mistakes and overlook important factors in a negotiation such as tone of voice, gestures, and body language. The videotape preserves such evidence for the purpose of constructive feedback.

Videotape feedback supervised by the instructor is extremely time-consuming, however. Therefore, it needs to be supplemented with supervised self-observation. A good way to accomplish this is to have students keep a journal of their negotiations inside and outside the classroom. They are encouraged to experiment with different approaches, and in the journal they analyze what tactics work well or poorly for them. After keeping a journal for a term, our trainees acquire the habit of constantly analyzing and critiquing their own performance in interactions. Finally, we expose them to a wide variety of negotiating situations—buying and selling, dealing with bosses and subordinates, negotiating and implementing a real estate contract, a corporate acquisition, collective bargaining, settling grievances, and various types of negotiations within and between groups.

Tailoring the learning experience to the unique needs of individuals provides the opportunity to address the special needs of women preparing for professional careers in organizations. For instance, the tendency for women to adopt a continuous time perspective can be a considerable asset in some bargaining situations and a liability in others. It is an asset when relationship-oriented, cooperative, and empathic behavior elicits similar behavior from the other party and leads to mutual accommodation. The liability of this time perspective is that it can make the negotiator vulnerable to exploitation by someone who seeks only short-term gain. In short, the woman who is too nice can be ripped off by an unscrupulous opponent.

The need to adapt to different approaches of the other party requires women to develop flexibility in their negotiating approaches. In practice this means that we encourage women to begin with a positive approach but to be ready to fight fire with fire if they encounter an exploitative, unyielding stance. Specifically, we hope to develop the woman's skill at expressing her commitment to a longer-term relationship and persuading the other person of the advantages of this predisposition. If this gentle persuasion doesn't work, she might interrupt the flow of the negotiation to comment on what is going on between the two people. She may approach this by trying to reflect back the position and assumptions of the other person. ("Let me see if I understand where you're coming from. You need to show your boss that you've gotten a good deal, and if you do that, I'm going to look bad to my boss. So why don't we brainstorm some ideas for how we can both look good?") If this positive approach does not work, the woman needs to have a more hard-line approach available, to use as a deterrent to the tactics of a chronically episodic-oriented opponent.

Another example of the ways in which women can constructively adapt their instinctive approaches to negotiation situations is to capitalize on their natural tendency to be empathic—that is, to be able to understand the perspective of the other party. Empathic tendencies give rise to empathy ("I'd like to learn what you would like to achieve by means of this agreement"), which can elicit a wealth of information about the interests of the other party. An empathic appeal is one of the most effective tactics that can be used to exert influence in a negotiation: it involves simply pointing out how settlements that are of benefit to oneself meet the other party's needs ("If we agree to what I suggested earlier, here's how *you'll* benefit").

We realize we may be coming close to suggesting ways to manipulate other people when we explain how to devise empathic appeals. Although it is true that information gained through empathic inquiries *could* be used exploitatively, such information also can be used in a way that ensures that both parties' needs are met and that both people feel good about the deal. Women's tendency to approach interactions from a continuous time perspective makes the manipulative use of information less likely.

The other feature of our development program that is worth mentioning attempts to undo some of the damage done during male socialization. Briefly, our mission is to help stamp out sports metaphors. This mission is as important to males whose thinking is distorted by these metaphors as it is to women who must suffer the effects.

Males become familiar with competitive games at an early age. When they encounter unfamiliar situations later on, they try to understand them in terms of what is familiar. As a result, many types of relationships are described in sports terms, from "making a big hit" in a business presentation to "scoring" on a date. Unfortunately, such metaphors shape the way males think about relationships in unhelpful ways. Sports contests are episodic by nature; they are either won or lost, so meeting mutual needs is inappropriate; any tactics that do not violate explicit rules are permissible; and the other person is defined as an opponent rather than a potential ally in solving a mutual problem.

It is very difficult to stamp out sports metaphors among negotiators. Because they so permeate the vocabulary of both men and women, they become invisible to those who are affected by them. Even some experts on negotiation cannot escape their effects. For example, some describe meeting mutual needs as a *win-win* solution, which stretches the metaphor beyond its logical limits: if there is a winner, someone else must be a loser; *both* people cannot win. Thus win-win imagery at best makes no sense and at worst perpetuates a view of the situation that fosters conflict rather than accommodation.

Summary

Our professional development programs have been considerably enriched by the research we have conducted on masculine-feminine differences in negotiating. Improvement of negotiating skills, properly guided by research findings, is vital as women endeavor to become more influential in settings traditionally dominated by their male counterparts. Negotiation skills also are vital as organizations take new forms, such as matrix management, increasingly complex structures, team-centered work forces, and Japanese-style management. All these innovations emphasize agreement and coordination between people, which in turn call for effective negotiation skills. Thus individuals should be strongly concerned with this aspect of their professional development, as should their higher-level managers.

A Note on the Study

The specific hypotheses we tested were based on our review of the literature and our experience in observing and training negotiators. We expected that individuals who are primarily feminine in their sex-role orientation would (1) tend to conceptualize interactions as continuous rather than episodic and (2) use negotiating tactics that strengthen the interpersonal relationship between the parties.

Our study used two different simulated business negotiations—an automobile purchase and a television advertising contract negotiation. Both were videotaped. The participants in the study (our experimental subjects) were sixty-four MBA students, all with previous business experience. Both men and women participated in the study, but the important variable was their sex-role orientation. As mentioned earlier, there is nothing in males' and females' genes or hormones that makes them negotiate differently; masculine-feminine differences arise from childhood socialization.

We measured sex-role orientation by means of a questionnaire.[6] Other personality characteristics were investigated in depth by a clinical psychologist, who used multiple measures to be sure to achieve a comprehensive assessment of each subject. Special instructions in the second simulation (the television advertising contract negotiation) informed subjects that they were in an episodic *situation*. Specifically, they were instructed that this was truly a one-shot deal; in fact, this was the last time they would be negotiating in this position for the company, and they would not be dealing with the other person again. This situation provided an opportunity to observe which subjects chose to respond to the situation by adopting an episodic *orientation* to their role and which subjects tried to maintain a continuous one.

The videotapes of the subjects' negotiating performance were analyzed by a trained observer, who was kept unaware of our hypotheses so that we could avoid possible biases to the analysis.

One of the clinical psychologist's specific tasks was to assess each subject's characteristic *tendency* to assume an episodic or a continuous orientation. In the one-hour, in-depth interview, he asked the subjects to describe various interactions they were having *outside* the laboratory study. From the patterns in the behavior they described, the psychologist was able to identify *general* tendencies to see situations as one-shot deals or as events within a long-term relationship.

In summary, then, we recruited sixty-four young professionals to participate in the study. Then we used a questionnaire to determine whether they had acquired a masculine or feminine sex-role orientation during their childhood socialization. Setting this information aside, we then asked the clinical psychologist to determine whether each person had a natural tendency to see negotiations as one-shot deals or as events in a longer-term relationship. Then we asked the participants to role-play two simulated negotiations each with a different (randomly assigned) partner. Videotapes of the negotiations were then analyzed to see what tactics were used. Finally, we put all the data together to see if, as we had hypothesized, the feminine negotiators had different time perspectives and used different tactics than their masculine counterparts.

Notes

1. See, for example, the following studies: M.S. Horner, "Toward an understanding of Achievement-Related Conflicts in Women," *Journal of Social Issues 28* (1972):157–175; N. Chodorow, "Family Structure and Feminine Personality," in M.Z. Rosaldo and L. Lamphere, eds., *Women, Culture and Society* (Stanford: Stanford University Press, 1974); J.B. Miller, *Toward a New Psychology of Women* (Boston: Beacon Press, 1976); C. Gilligan, *In a Different Voice* (Cambridge, Mass.: Harvard University Press, 1982).
2. See Chodorow, "Family Structure."
3. See E.E. Maccoby and C.N. Jacklin, *The Psychology of Sex Differences* (Stanford: Stanford University Press, 1974).
4. See K.M. Bartol and D.A. Butterfield, "Sex Effects in Evaluating Leaders," *Journal of Applied Psychology 61* (1976):446–454.
5. See J.Z. Rubin and B.R. Brown, *The Social Psychology of Bargaining and Negotiation* (New York: Academic Press, 1975).
6. The questionnaire was the Bem Sex-Role Inventory. For details of this measure, see S.L. Bem, "The Measurement of Psychological Androgyny," *Journal of Consulting and Clinical Psychology 42* (1974):155–162.

10

Balancing Acts: Work-Family Conflict and the Dual-Career Couple

Nicholas Beutell
Jeffrey Greenhaus

It may be that organizations of the future will have to pay attention to their effects on people other than employed persons (spouses, children) and allow the needs of families to influence organizational decisions and shape organizational policies. Questions about day care, part-time work, maternity and paternity leave, executive transfers, spousal involvement in career planning, and the treatment of family dysfunctions—all difficult to approach at present—may become primary considerations in the future.[1]

Increasingly, business organizations are expected to be socially responsible in their methods of operation, in their products and the services they provide and in their organization's policies. Recognizing the relationship between the organization, its employees and their families is a first step.[2]

One important by-product of the changing American workplace is an increasing awareness that employees' work and family lives are interdependent. The roles of women and men are changing, and so is the possibility of interference between work and family responsibilities. The blurring of the boundaries between work and family is highlighted by increasing numbers of dual-career and dual-earner couples (many with children) in the work force. Concerns over balancing work and family life are especially important for professional women, since research has shown that women frequently continue to do the bulk of home maintenance activities in addition to their career pursuits.[3] Even female physicians (who might be expected to be highly involved in their careers) report no reduction in household participation and responsibility. It is clear that additional research and discussion are needed in order to help professional women and men in dual-career couples cope with the strains of balancing their work and family lives.

Despite many changes in role attitudes and patterns of labor force participation, a recent study found that only 20 percent of the companies surveyed perceived the dual-career couple as a problem from the company's point of view.[4] These results may reflect, in part, the reluctance of organizations to deal with their employees' family lives. That would be unfortunate, since excessive conflict between work and family roles can adversely affect employees' feelings of well-being and might contribute to their leaving the organization.

The emergence of the dual-career couple may be associated with additional stresses for women. As some researchers have noted:

> While the dual-career lifestyle offers women the potential of pursuing both career and family interests, it also presents difficulties and challenges not found in the traditional marriage . . . such as role conflict, role overload, and conflicts surrounding involvement in and the priority of career pursuits. Although such difficulties exist, however, continued facilitation of women's involvement and satisfaction in careers necessitates greater understanding of the means by which the dual-career lifestyle can be successfully managed and maintained [pp. 242–243].[5]

A discussion of work–family conflict may be helpful in this regard.

Work–Family Conflict

One way to view your work and family lives is in terms of interference or conflict. When you feel the strains of competing work and family demands, you are experiencing work–family conflict. The more you concentrate on work (or on family) activities, the more diffciult it is to respond to family (or work) demands.[6] Three different forms of work–family conflict occur: (1) time-based, (2) strain-based, and (3) behavior-based. We will define briefly each type of work–family conflict:

1. *Time-based conflict* refers to your use of limited time resources. Time spent working generally cannot be devoted to family activities, and vice versa. Caring for a sick child, for example, may prevent you from going to the office to complete an important project. Similarly, staying late at the office may make it difficult to have dinner with your family at the customary hour. Extensive time commitment to work and/or family roles can produce conflict.

2. *Strain-based conflict* refers to the spillover of strain generated in one role into your performance in another role. If you experience a great deal of strain because of extensive work demands, for example, you may find it difficult to be an attentive parent or spouse at home. Similarly, strain originating from your family roles as parent and/or spouse may keep you from doing a good job at work.

3. *Behavior-based conflict* refers to the notion that each us has differing sets of behaviors (one set of behaviors for work and separate set for family) that may be incompatible. If you are a manager in a business corporation, aggressiveness and objectivity may be expected for successful job performance. Yet at home, warmth and nurturance may be viewed as more appropriate behaviors by your spouse and children. If you find it difficult to shift gears from one role to another, you may experience conflict between work and family responsibilities.

One interesting issue is whether or not men and women experience role pressures and strains in the same way. This question has many practical implications, since both spouses are subject to many role pressures. Some research indicates that men and women in dual-career couples do view their work and family lives quite similarly.[7] This does not mean that men and women are equally likely to experience the same levels and types of work–family conflicts. We feel that more research evidence is necessary in order to conclude that there are no differences in such perceptions or in work–family conflicts. Traditionally, however, women have had stronger pressures to conform to family role demands over work demands, whereas the reverse has been true for men. Clearly, traditional role attitudes have changed dramatically, but the extent of actual changes in role behavior is not known.

There are many sources of work–family conflict among women and men. Understanding the forces that contribute to each type (time, strain, behavior) of work–family conflict has important implications for the management of human resources in general and for professional women and men in dual-career couples in particular. We will explore some of these implications, indicating the type(s) of work–family conflict that are involved.

Implications for the Management of Human Resources

Perhaps the most general implication is the need for organizations to recognize the potential for interference between work and family roles among professional women and men. Recognition of the problems associated with work–family conflict is, of course, only the first step. We need to find new ways of balancing work and family demands. Organizational strategies for successful role integration need to be developed, examined, and modified where necessary. A wide variety of organizational practices and policies may help individuals in dual-career families to manage work and family:

1. The presentation of realistic information.

2. The development of flexible work patterns.

3. Job redesign.

4. The establishment of support services.

5. An integrated career planning/human resource management system.

Realistic Information

The presentation of balanced, realistic information to job candidates has received a lot of attention from organizational researchers. It is generally believed that people who have a realistic idea of both the good and the bad aspects of their new jobs will be happier and will be more likely to stay with the job than if their expectations had been too high. The need to possess realistic information, however, is not limited to people outside an organization or to new employees. Research has found, for example, that many middle managers possessed inadequate information regarding future career opportunities within the organization.[8] Managers who had been with the company for a long time did not necessarily have more adequate information than relative newcomers.

Different job assignment sequences (or career paths) will undoubtedly differ in the degree of stress and time commitment involved; the extent to which the occupation defines family life and demands the involvement of other family members; and the amount of travel required—in short, many of the conditions that may affect on work–family conflict. Therefore, employees need to know a great deal about organizational career opportunities. Just as realistic job previews have been suggested for entry positions within an organization, so realistic information about jobs in alternative career options can help professional women and men make informed career decisions that are consistent with work, family, and personal values. For example, if the next apparently logical position on your career path involves a relocation to a distant city, realistic information could help you decide whether such a move is in line with your total life situation.

In order to provide realistic information about alternative career paths, your organization needs to collect the appropriate information and then provide a way for people to get the information. The first need highlights the importance of rigorous analyses of your company's jobs to identify the distinctive characteristics of each position or group of positions. Such information can be compiled and used by human resource specialists and line managers to counsel employees. Indeed, realistic information may be particularly important if you are a professional woman who may be a pioneer—one of the first few women in your career field. Such information could help you make choices that make balancing your work and family a little easier.

Accurate information also makes the work world more predictable, which in turn may reduce the strain associated with career transitions. For example, one study found that managers' relocations went more smoothly when the transfer was anticipated and when the managers were well-informed about the nature of the new job.[9] In short, accurate information may help employees' career decision making and reduce work-produced strain.

Organizational Flexibility

Since a considerable amount of work–family conflict is the result of time-based incompatibility, it is reasonable to assume that flexible work schedules can benefit employees who attempt to balance simultaneous role demands. If you have additional flexibility in scheduling your work hours, you may find it easier to cope with your family pressures. There is some support for the idea that so-called flexitime programs can lessen such conflicts.[10] Flexitime schedules are intended to give employees choices in the timing of work and nonwork activities. A flexitime program includes a core time when employees must be at work and a flexible time that gives them freedom to choose the remaining hours of work. A thorough examination of a flexitime program in the federal government produced some unexpected results. The flexitime program appeared to ease the work–family conflict of only certain groups of employees: men whose wives were not employed, married women without children, and single men. The people most in need of help—women with major family responsibilities—did not experience less work–family conflict under the flexitime program than under a standard time program.

These researchers concluded that the flexitime program they investigated was not far-reaching enough to help those people with primary child-care responsibilities. Another interpretation is also possible. A standard time schedule provides a regular structure to work activities. A flexitime program may actually introduce additional stresses for people with major family responsibilities. First, you must schedule work hours on a daily or weekly basis during the hours when family demands are likely to be the highest (for example, late afternoon when children come home from school). Second, family members may attempt to use the flexibility in your work schedule to assert additional demands. Flexitime programs may highlight rather than reduce work–family conflict for such high-family-demand employees.

A number of authors have suggested more fundamental changes in work schedules to help employees manage the work–family interface: permanent part-time work, job sharing, sabbaticals, parental work leaves, allowing both husband and wife to work for the same company, shortened work weeks, and alternating periods of work and family over the course of a person's life. Whether these programs would, in fact, reduce work–family conflict has not been determined. Such programs should receive additional research attention since they appear to be well suited to some of the role dilemmas faced by dual-career couples. Indeed, such programs may benefit your organization in terms of increased job satisfaction and productivity.

Job Redesign

Job redesign—the alteration of jobs to increase productivity and quality of work life of employees—has come to be synonymous with rehumanizing the workplace. Redesigning jobs can be one way of improving life at work as well as life outside of work. There is some evidence that people employed in nonchallenging, repetitive jobs experience high levels of work–family conflict.[11] It has been suggested that nonchallenging jobs have the strongest separation from family life and, therefore, that people in these positions are more likely to experience conflict between work and family. Redesigning jobs to ensure a better fit between your skill and abilities and the requirements of your job may prove useful in reducing the negative impact of work on family life. We need to figure out a way to determine the appropriate level of job demands, consistent with an employee's abilities and aspirations.

There is also evidence that stressful work situations can produce work–family conflict. Adjustments in work stressors—shorter working hours, less travel, less ambiguity and conflict, fewer activities where employees represent their company to the outside world—should reduce the degree of work–family conflict experienced by dual-career couples. Indeed, it has been argued that proper attention to a balance between work and family is indicative of a high quality of work life. The quality-of-work-life approach is is characterized by job involvement, feelings of self-control and responsibility, and reduced levels of stress.

The Establishment of Support Systems

It is unlikely that job stress can (or should) be eliminated. Stress is almost inevitable for employees who are highly involved in demanding work careers, and a certain amount of stress is necessary for peak performance. Organizational boundaries must be crossed, travel is essential on many occasions, new jobs require major adjustments, and a certain level of ambiguity and conflict is probably inherent in many managerial and professional positions. If work stressors cannot be eradicated completely, employees will need help in managing stress successfully.

Two researchers described a seminar designed to strengthen employees' (and spouses') analytical and problem-solving skills regarding travel-related stress.[12] These researchers concluded that the seminar increased problem-solving effectiveness for many participants. Such workshops can be applied to a wide range of work–family issues. For example, problem-solving programs for students and their spouses have begun to address the balance of work and family roles. Peer groups at different career stages can be formed to discuss problems of balancing work and family. Finally, organizations need to recognize the role of supportive spouses in the career development of professional women and men. Your spouse can be a particularly important source of support in dealing with role stress. It has been suggested that spouses visit their wives and husbands at work so they have a better understanding of various job demands. You might want to see if your organization offers such programs.

In addition to developing programs to help employees cope with stress and conflict, organizations may help meet employees' child-care needs more directly. Researchers have outlined a number of child-care strategies, including in-house day care, after-school programs, care for sick children, and vouchers for parents to pay for the type of child care they find most appropriate.[13] These researchers have argued that the voucher system is the most viable child-care option for organizations. Employees would be reimbursed for all or part of their expenses. You should find out whether child-care vouchers are included in your company's benefits package.

There has been a dramatic increase in the number of employee assistance programs offered by organizations. Employee assistance programs are intended to help employees with personal problems that hinder their job performance, attendance, or off-the-job behaviors. Typical problems handled by employee assistance counselors might be alcoholism or marital problems. Though intended primarily for other problems, employee assistance programs also can play a role in diagnosing excessive work–family conflict in the lives of professional women and men. If you are reluctant to discuss problems involving family activities, your manager will play a critical role in the diagnostic referral process. One writer has suggested that managers look for symptoms suggesting stress. In-house counseling or referral to community sources may be useful for acute conflicts.

Integration of Career and Human Resource Systems

Most of the critical conflicts between work and family come at career path junctures, where major changes in lifestyle are likely to occur. A delicate balance of concession and demand must be achieved to keep employees and their families loyal and committed. Many major employers operate as though there is only one breadwinner in the family. They interpret an employee's reluctance to leap at an advancement opportunity as evidence of disloyalty.[14]

In the broadest sense, the successful integration of work and family roles requires a human resource planning and development system that is consistent with individual career/life goals. This system would include:

1. A greater incorporation of life planning activities in career planning programs: If your company has a career planning program, you might want to see whether life planning is included. This approach recognizes that family goals, leisure, and personal interests are important factors in the career planning process. At Hewlett-Packard, for example, participants in the career workshops complete a questionnaire titled "Couples Career and Lifestyle." Both partners independently fill out the questionnaire and then discuss needs and conflicts. This approach seems well suited to the role dilemmas of dual-career couples.

2. More accurate information about your organization in general and the personal consequences of alternative career paths in particular: Such information would help people make career choices consistent with their achievement needs and their family needs.

3. More flexibility in the selection of your career moves: Frequently people get locked into a position that is no longer challenging or fulfilling. Unfortunately, it is difficult to break out of this situation. Additional flexibility would broaden the view of career

success beyond climbing the corporate ladder as an end in itself toward effective performance, pride, and psychological success.

4. Realistic performance feedback and an open dialogue between you and your manager on important work and family issues.

5. The inclusion of employee values and aspirations on inventories used to counsel employees.

6. More effective assessment techniques for selecting and promoting job candidates and for providing useful feedback to employees.

Individual Strategies for Coping with Work-Family Conflict

The human resource implications of work–family conflict have been discussed. Certainly individuals also need to be concerned about dealing with such stressors. In this section we will look at some of the things that you can do when your role pressures become too intense.

Coping strategies are techniques intended to reduce or eliminate the pressures that cause stress. Two general types of coping strategies can be identified: (1) those that change the objective situation causing the stress (for example, you and your manager renegotiate your job duties to make them more compatible with your family responsibilities); and (2) those that change your perceptions and feelings about the conflict (for example, your self-imposed standards for being a successful parent were too high and negatively affected your job performance—you can lower your standards and still be a good parent). Alcohol, drugs, and excessive television viewing are common behavioral responses to work and family stresses. Unfortunately, these behaviors may cover up stress temporarily but can actually increase stress in the long run. Use of such *avoidance behaviors* does not change the situation that caused the stress, nor do such activities change your feelings about the stressors. We believe that successful coping strategies change either the stressful situation or your feelings about and perceptions of the stressful situation, and thereby reduce stress to an acceptable level.

We will identify a coping strategy for each of the three types of work–family conflict identified earlier: time, strain, and behavior. There are numerous coping strategies and individual coping styles, and it is not possible to discuss all of them here. The following examples suggest some types of things you can do to manage your stress.

Time-Based Conflict

Many individuals in dual-career families feel they simply do not have enough time to be all-star employees, spouses, parents, friends, community members, and so on. There are so many demands and so few hours in the day. Since it is unlikely that the number of hours in a day will increase in the near future, the hours we do have should be used to good advantage. The efficient use of time is frequently called *time management*. Time management involves setting priorities for your daily activities. This can be accomplished by making a list of things to do and then deciding which items deserve the most time and attention. Time should be scheduled for high-priority items, with some open time for emergencies and unexpected events. Flexibility is required. Prioritizing your activities helps you to avoid spinning your wheels on time-consuming but relatively unproductive things. It is a good idea to write out your list and check your progress at the end of the day. This feedback should help you plan subsequent days more effectively and realistically.

Strain-Based Conflict

The spillover of strain to work or family is very common. To cope with this situation, you must first identify the stressors that are creating the conflict. Next you must decide which stressors can be altered or modified. Depending on your particular interpersonal style, you can attempt to change the situation causing the stressors, your reaction to the stressors, or both. For example, if your boss schedules important meetings in the late afternoon, when you are most concerned about family responsibilities or nonwork commitments, you might be able to convince your boss to schedule such meetings at other times. It is also possible that your concern over family stressors is out of proportion to the reality of the situation. In that case, perhaps you can be more attentive to your meetings.

Behavior-Based Conflict

The key issue in behavior-based conflict is shifting gears and winding down from work to family roles. The transition from family to work also needs to be considered. It is the abruptness of the transition that seems to be problematic. Individuals must be aware of the transition dynamics to effectively manage their stress. Here are some things that you can do to manage the transition period:

1. Make a conscious effort to lighten up at the end of the work day rather than being maximally involved in work at the last minute.

2. Plan your work into manageable units so you have a sense of closure or completeness when the work day is done. Don't be preoccupied with unfinished work when you're at home. Also, reward yourself when you complete each part of a project.

3. Do not attempt to undo or redo actions and decisions made during your day. Resist the temptation to rehash your behaviors; move on to something else instead.

4. Plan a home or after-work activity so that you don't experience a letdown from an intense day at work. Ideally, this activity would be distinct from the kinds of things you do at work, and also something you enjoy.

It is important to point out that these are only examples of the kinds of strategies that might reduce stress. Each individual must experiment to find the strategies that work.

Summary

We have suggested a number of realistic steps that organizations and individuals can take to reduce the likelihood of work–family conflict, as well as strategies for coping with conflict when it does occur. It is particularly important for human resource managers to be aware of the different types of work–family conflict and the role of family life in various personnel policies. It is also important for professional women and men in dual-career couples to be aware of organizational practices and the types of coping strategies they can use to manage their stress. Individuals and families have shouldered the responsibility for work–family conflict in the past. Carefully planned human resource strategies (and, from an individual perspective, successful coping strategies) are now needed to help dual-career couples balance their work and family lives successfully.

Notes

1. R.M. Kanter, *Work and Family in the United States: A Critical Review and Agenda for Research and Policy.* (New York: Russell Sage Foundation, 1977), p. 3.
2. J.S. Hunsaker, "Work and Family Must Be Integrated," *Personnel Administrator 28,* no. 4 (1983):89.
3. M. Heins, S. Smock, J. Jacobs, and M. Stein, "Productivity of Women Physicians," *Journal of the American Medical Association 236* (1976):1961–1964.
4. R.E. Kopelman, L. Rosenweig, and L.H. Lally, "Dual-Career Couples: The Organizational Response," *Personnel Administrator 27,* no. 9 (1982):73–78.
5. S.A. Hardesty and N.E. Betz, "The Relationships of Career Salience, Attitudes toward Women, and Demographic and Family Characteristics to Marital Adjustment in Dual-Career Couples," *Journal of Vocational Behavior 17* (1980):242–243.
6. J.H. Greenhaus and N.J. Beutell, "Sources of Conflict between Work and Family Roles," *Academy of Management Review 10* (1985):76–88.
7. U. Sekaran, "How Husbands and Wives in Dual-Career Families Perceive Their Family and Work Worlds," *Journal of Vocational Behavior 22* (1983):228–302.
8. J.H. Greenhaus and H.K. Springob, "Managerial Perceptions of Career Planning Information," *Journal of Management 6* (1980):79–88.
9. J.M. Brett and J.D. Werbel, *The Effect of Job Transfers on Employees and Their Families* (Washington, D.C.: Employee Relocation Council, 1980).
10. H.C. Bohen and A. Viveros-Long, *Balancing Jobs and Family Life: Do Flexible Work Schedules Help?* (Philadelphia: Temple University Press, 1981).
11. A.P. Jones and M.C. Butler, "A Role Transition Approach to the Stresses of Organizationally Induced Family Role Disruptions," *Journal of Marriage and the Family 42* (1980):367–376.
12. S.A. Culbert and J.R. Renshaw, "Coping with the Stresses of Travel as an Opportunity for Improving the Quality of Work and Family Life," *Family Process 11* (1972):321–337.
13. S.E. LaMarre and K. Thompson, "Industry-Sponsored Day Care," *Personnel Administrator 29,* no. 2 (1984):53–66.
14. Hunsaker, "Work and Family," p. 89.

References

Hall, D.T., and Hall, F.S. 1976. "What's New in Career Management?" *Organizational Dynamics* 5:17–23.

Hall, F.S., and Hall, D.T. 1979. *The Two-Career Couple*. Reading, Mass.: Addison-Wesley.

Hoffman, L.W., and Nye, R.I. 1974. *Working Mothers*. San Francisco: Jossey-Bass.

London, M., and Stumpf, S.A. 1982. *Managing Careers*. Reading, Mass.: Addison-Wesley.

Louis, M.R. 1980. "Career Transitions: Varieties and Commonalities." *Academy of Management Review* 5:329–340.

Pesco, M. 1982. "Stress Management: Separating Myth from Reality." *Personnel Administrator* 27:57–67.

Schein, E.H. 1978. *Career Dynamics: Matching Individual and Organizational Needs*. Reading, Mass.: Addison-Wesley.

Walton, R.E. 1973. "Quality of Working Life: What Is It?" *Sloan Management Review* 15:11–21.

Wanous, J.P. 1980. *Organizational Entry*. Reading, Mass.: Addison-Wesley.

11

Successful Women in a Man's World: The Myth of Managerial Androgyny

Mark Lipton

By any criteria, Karen Valenstein has made it as a corporate woman. At thirty-eight, she is a first vice-president at E.F. Hutton & Company and one of the most powerful women in investment banking. Her annual salary is reportedly a quarter of a million dollars,[1] she is respected and admired by her peers and superiors, and she closes enormous deals that leave competitors at other investment houses scratching their heads. Married for fourteen years and the mother of two children, she lives in Manhattan and manages to put in volunteer hours at the Metropolitan Museum of Art. Her job, however, takes a clear priority over most of the rest of her life, and she devotes an astounding number of hours each week to it.

With male colleagues she can comfortably maintain a patter of conversation heavily peppered with barnyard language. She's never flustered by a vulgar joke. On Monday mornings, Karen knows the football scores. When meetings with colleagues and clients run late into the night at local saloons, she keeps up with the best of them.

Some women struggle to assimilate their personality to the aggressive, hostile, politicized environment found in the most highly competitive corporations. There are those, however, like Karen Valenstein, who fit—and feel that the fit is quite natural. One of Ms. Valenstein's colleagues at the First Boston Corporation summed up his admiration for her: "Let's put it this way: You'd like to have someone walk into your office the way Karen does and chew off the corner of your desk. Not every male has that quality, and not every woman has it."

Women encounter an array of obstacles as they scale the hierarchies of corporations. Faced with these obstacles, some women falter, some are pushed out, some lose the drive to continue climbing—and some succeed, rising to meet the challenge. What can we learn from the women who do succeed? Do they have characteristics that differentiate them from those who do not clear the obstacles? Do some women encounter more obstacles in their path than others? This chapter will explore these questions and will elaborate on some characteristics of successful corporate women. The very mechanism that allows the characteristics to surface, and makes some women "acceptable" as managers, may, it will be seen, hinder the performance of these same women.

Before discussing women like Karen Valenstein, we might find it helpful to take a step back and look at organizations more generally. Research conducted during the past decade provides increasing evidence that organizations can take on some very human characteristics. The concept of *corporate culture* supports this notion by reminding us that organizations are made up of people. Since these people have their own individual personalities, it is reasonable to assume that an organization represents some type of collective personality, although it certainly may not represent all the individual personalities combined.

If each organization has a unique personality, it is not unreasonable to attach to it yet another human characteristic: gender. For example: if Ma Bell was, in fact, a woman, what might we call her today? AT&T is now restructured and trying to succeed in a highly competitive environment. Along the road from virtual monopoly to razor-sharp competitor, however, Ma Bell's gender seemed to change. When we hear stock analysts describe AT&T as a "lean, mean fighting machine," the phrase does not conjure up the image of a maternalistic Ma Bell.

Other areas of research have explored how people perceive the idea of effective management. What is an effective manager? What characteristics do we believe effective mangers possess? How do they behave?

Successful Manager = Man

Dr. Virginia Schein found that certain words emerge when managers are asked to describe the idea of effective management. In one study, 500 managers of both sexes were asked to describe, in single words or phrases, their perceptions of *successful managers, men,* and *women.* She found that the respondents saw men and successful managers as possessing the characteristics of leadership ability, competitiveness, self-confidence, objectivity, aggressiveness, forcefulness, and a desire for responsibility. These terms were used to describe effective managers and men *separately.* Women were perceived as possessing extremely different characteristics, which will be discussed later in this chapter. Similar studies have subsequently supported the same conclusions: both men and women have a very strong preference for a "masculine" manager, and most respondents characterize a good manager in strongly masculine terms. Indeed, research conducted by the Gallup organization and *The Wall Street Journal* in November 1984 reaffirmed that both male and female executives prefer to have men as bosses.[2]

This theme has been carried through in still other findings: for example, when managers were asked to make managerial selection decisions on the basis of sex, they tended to decide in favor of males. Other studies have found that males, compared to females, were more likley to be selected into a supposedly male-oriented position, whereas females rather than males were more likely to be selected for a female-oriented position. Management was considered a male-oriented position, whereas many nonmangement jobs such as health care worker (but not physician) and teacher tended to have female orientations. In other words, when both male and female managers were asked to *think* "manager," they responded in masculine terms.

Even physical characteristics tie into this theme. Women are often placed on a feminine-masculine continuum on the basis of features such as body shape, stature, hair texture, voice, and facial hair. Short, blond, long-haired, blue-eyed women are at the more feminine end of the scale; tall, thin, short-dark-haired women are at the more masculine end. Feminine women are often stereotyped as more fragile, helpless, and sexually attractive than more masculine women. Overall, women in traditionally male jobs (including management) tend to be taller and thinner than average and tend to have short, dark hair.[3]

Reproducible Characteristics

One rationale for this preference is that men accept women with masculine features or characteristics more readily than they do women with feminine features. Rosabeth Kanter noted in her book *Men and Women of the Corporation* that all managers, regardless of gender, tend to be extremely protective of any source of acquired power. They carefully guard their power and will share it and any special privileges only with those whom they perceive as fitting in. When we give our trust to people in organizations, we seek out those like ourselves. We depend on our *observations* of how people behave to help us determine whether they are the right sort of person. We want to make sure that the ones we choose to work with, the ones with whom we share this power, are "our kind of people."

In an environment like Wall Street, where Karen Valenstein works, a word heard often is *fit*. Can you *fit* into the team dynamics of the company? Is there a *fit* between you and the clients who provide the additional business, which is also the ultimate measurement for success and compensation?

People who manage, especially men, often reproduce themselves through subtle, unconscious promotion criteria. In the early 1960s Wilbert Moore described this concept as "homosexual reproduction"—men reproducing themselves in their own image. In the past, executives made sure the men they hired as their direct subordinates came from backgrounds similar to their own. The type of college they attended, the branch of the armed forces in which they served, and interest in similar sports were all important factors for promising executives. Such criteria still exist, but they have become simultaneously more complex and more subtle as women and other minority groups have come to populate managerial ranks. There *are* reproducible characteristics, which explains why some women can climb the corporate ladder while others remain stuck on the lower rungs.

An impressive body of research continually reinforces the belief that *effective management* is perceived as having a gender: male. In organizations where existing management is dominated by males, my own research has strongly suggested that a women can possess certain traits that might increase her chances of being hired or promoted into the management group. As noted previously, she can look more masculine than feminine; but also, perhaps more important, she can *behave* more masculine than feminine.

What is considered masculine behavior? Interestingly, a concept that evolved from medical research describes certain behaviors and characteristics that are highly related to heart disease. Many of these characteristics are identical to those that make up the notion that we have come to know as *masculinity*.

One predictor of coronary heart disease (CHD) is a concept known as the *coronary-prone behavior pattern,* more commonly referred to as *Type A behavior.* Type A represents actual behavior, things we can watch people do if we consciously observe them. In the extreme, it includes a chronic sense of rushing and making the most of every minute, a hard-driving, competitive orientation which usually includes some hostility. Type A individuals have a strong dislike for being idle and a chronic impatience with people and situations that are seen as blocking their efforts to get things accomplished. Type B individuals, by contrast, tend to be more relaxed and easygoing, less hostile, and less overtly competitive. They are not necessarily less motivated to achieve, but they seldom experience an anxious feeling of wasting time when not engaged in clearly productive activities.

Type A is not an absolute concept; it is not something you have entirely or not at all. No one is typically Type A 100 percent of the time. Some people exhibit an extraordinary number of Type A characteristics and very few Type B characteristics, but it is always a matter of degree. Most people exhibit some aspects of both types of behavior. If you were to be assessed as one type (either A or B), however, you would rarely exhibit intense, consistent behaviors of the *other* type over a period of time. The behaviors that make up Type A are very stable over time. This makes people quite predictable from a scientific research standpoint, but it is difficult for the individuals themselves if they desire to change.

Effective Management = Men = Masculinity = Type A

Some very standardized words have been used to describe the concepts behind the idea of Type A behavior. Table 11–1 lists a number of these words, but, beyond mere words, people exhibiting strong Type A behaviors *are aggressive, competitive, ambitious, hostile, needing to be in control, punctual,* and *perfectionists.* The column of terms representing behaviors that describe the concept of masculinity was developed by Sandra Bem after exhaustive studies in this area.[4] If we look at the research that explores how people perceive *men* in organizations and how they also perceive *effective managers,* we find that *they use almost the same terminology.* Not surprisingly, the terminology these people used to describe *effective managers* and *men* also describes the notion of *masculinity.* We

Table 11–1

*Similarity of Terminology Between
Type A Behavior and Sex-Role Stereotyping*

Adjectives Describing the Perceived Characteristics of Femininity	Adjectives Describing the Perceived Characteristics of Masculinity	Adjectives Describing the Perceived Characteristics of Men in Organizations and/or Effective Management	Type A Behavioral Characteristics
Yielding	Aggressive	Aggressive	Aggressive
Cheerful	Competitive	Competitive	Competitive
Shy	Ambitious	Ambitious	Ambitious
Affectionate	Forceful	Forceful	Hostile
Sympathetic	Willing to take stand	Desirous of responsibility	Need for control
Feminine	Assertive	Punctuality	Punctuality
Compassionate	Self-reliant	Precision	Perfectionism
Soft-spoken	Independent		
Warm	Has leadership ability		
Tender	Takes risks		
Gullible	Makes decisions easily		
Childlike	Self-sufficient		
Gentle	Dominant		
Loyal	Masculine		
Soothes feelings	Acts as leader		
Avoids harsh language	Individualistic		
Loves children	Defends own beliefs		
Sensitive to others	Athletic		
Flatterable	Strong personality		
Understanding	Analytical		

perceive effective managers as men, and the men as being masculine, while at the same time perceiving Type A behavior as a collection of masculine characteristics.

In any discussion of masculinity and feminity, we must also consider a third concept that exists when both are combined: *androgyny.* In contrast to the other two, an androgynous sex role represents an *equal* amount of both masculine and feminine attributes.

The concept of Type A was developed to help us understand what causes coronary heart disease. When we isolate many Type A behaviors, however, we find behaviors identical to those that describe the notion of masculinity. If you are assessed as being high on the Type A scale, the odds are considerable that you also exhibit many so-called masculine characteristics, fewer androgynous ones, and still fewer feminine characteristics.

Some authors, such as Alice Sargent in her book *The Androgynous Manager,* suggest that the best managers are androgynous and that this is the inevitable wave of the future. In this context effective managers are perceived as acting in both masculine and feminine ways. In particular, she suggests that effective managers, whether male or female, must assume certain behaviors that are characterized as feminine and others that are typically masculine. It would be encouraging to think that the concepts of masculinity and femininity can work side by side and, by so doing, will make organizations even more productive. We would like to believe that women pushing through the barriers at high levels in organizations are representative of most other women. Unfortunately, it seems that these beliefs are not being fulfilled as predicted. If this is indeed the case, then women moving into or trying to move into executive ranks are, as we will see, faced with an array of potential longer-term problems.

In the United States, the proportion of men who are Type A is perhaps greater than in any other country in the world, with only Japan and Germany as possible contenders. In contrast, women are typically Type B, with a much smaller minority, compared to men, who would be classified as Type A. Generally, women are not as aggressive, competitive, rushed, hostile, or in need of being in control as men appear to be. Not coincidentally, women also do not suffer from as high an incidence of heart disease. Only a small minority of women in the United States, therefore, would be classified as intensely Type A.

Groups of executive women whom I have studied have proved to be considerably more Type A when compared to women in the general population of the United States. That is, when successful corporate women were assessed for Type A personalities, the proportion classified as intensely Type A was far greater than the proportion of intensely Type A women in general. In fact, the proportion of successful women in corporations who are Type A is about equal to the proportion of their male corporate counterparts who are Type A. These findings indicate that the group of women who have moved up the corporate ladder are just as Type A as their male corporate counterparts, but far more likely to be Type A than other women. Clearly, this indicates a preference in these organizations for Type A women.

The phenomenon that seems to emerge from these findings relates back to the notions of reproducible characteristics and *fit*. Type A behavior is probably one of the few unconscious ways in which a man can feel that a certain woman is, in some respect, similar to him. Type A behavior makes her seem more masculine to her male counterparts and increases the probability of her being included with other men, by being hired or promoted into an upper management group. She fits with the group of men and the highly competitive environment.

For the woman, also, this is unconscious and unplanned. Type A behavior is established in a human being by the time he or she is a teenager. You don't go from being a strong Type B to a strong Type A just by working for a fast-paced organization or by getting clues that being Type A will allow you to fit in better. In some cases an organization can certainly fuel Type A behavior, but only *if* the personality factors are in place. For example, Type As find themselves in their element when their company overschedules their days, demands a total commitment to the job at the expense of family and other interests, and requires that all projects be completed by yesterday. It is very important to realize, however, that the corporation cannot *make* you Type A. If its culture supports this, it can regard you more favorably if you seem Type A, it can reward you for behaving in a Type A manner, but it cannot turn you into a type A.

Some organizations more than others try to recruit individuals who are Type A and reward those who act in a Type A fashion. Not only has fast career development been found to be related to Type A, but the prevalence of Type As in an organization also seems to be related to company growth rate.[5] The faster people move up the ladder in a company and/or the faster the growth rate of the company, the more Type As you should expect to find at managerial levels. So, when you take a look around your organization for the prevalence of Type As, ask yourself two questions:

First, is the organization growing at a faster-than-average rate compared to others in its industry or compared to similar industries? This is a good rule of thumb for estimating a larger percentage of Type As. In the banking industry, Citibank, the fastest growing top-ten firm for the past decade, would meet this criterion. Not surprisingly, being Type A at this organization helps. In the same way that individuals are characterized as Type A, so too can we generalize about organizations. The more an organization expects and reinforces Type A–like behavior from its management, the more we can describe its corporate culture as Type A.[6]

Second, who are the movers and shakers in your organization—the ones climbing the ladder faster than others? Chances are they will be more Type A than others and may expect those around them to be Type A. If this individual is a man, a female subordinate would be likely to be required to possess Type A characteristics.

Women and Masculinity

In a variety of studies, other characteristics tend to emerge as being common among female *executives,* though not necessarily among females in general. In addition they experience higher levels of the need for power and a higher level of self-esteem than their nonmanagerial counterparts. In these respects, they are more similar to the men in those positions than to other women who have not chosen to aspire to managerial levels.

One conclusion to be drawn from this is that women have to act masculine if they are going to fit and succeed in the man's world of competitive corporate life. Karen Valenstein's first boss at E.F. Hutton, for example, offered her early advice: "I'm not going to pay you like a broad, and I'm not going to treat you like a broad, so don't act like a broad." Type A behavior is the acceptable way for a woman to act masculine. In a variety of studies where Type A was not assessed, women assessed as masculine were found to be more extroverted than feminine or androgynous women.[7] Extroversion is considered a necessary personality prerequisite for management. Masculine women were the first to assume leadership positions in group problem-solving experiments and characterized as leadership-oriented. They were also found to be least dependent on others, least submissive in their daily interactions, and most demanding of others, when compared to feminine or androgynous women.

The Paradox of the Type A Woman Manager

There are two internal forces, among others, that influence the Type A female manager. The first is a need to prove her worth, to satisfy her need for achievement by succeeding in the face of challenge. Second is the acceptance by an overwhelmingly male decision-making structure, which perceives Type A women as more similar to themselves than to other women. The Type A woman has the strength and drive to battle a range of barriers placed before her. The Type B woman may not see these obstacles as appealing; she may choose other, more consistent options for her life or other arenas for achievement. For example, a Type B woman could possibly derive greater satisfaction from raising a family and caring for a home as a means to fulfilling her need for achievement. Type As perceive barriers as challenges, whereas Type Bs may see barriers as antagonistic and problematic. The Type A woman is not simply a survivor, she is a winner at the organizational game. She sees daily organizational problems as challenges to test her limits. She plays to win.

Although she is winning at this game, however, she is doing so at a cost. The few women who enjoy high-status positions are often subjected to male-dominated policymaking, and they experience stresses and strain not felt by their male peers. For example, feelings of isolation, conflicting demands between career and marriage and family, and coping with prejudice and discrimination are often reported by these women. Indeed, research conducted in 1980 found that managerial women who are Type A perceive themselves as undergoing higher levels of stress than their Type B counterparts, with frustration, irritation, and anxiety being the three psychological symptoms most frequently identified.[8]

Although Type A may be one of the prerequisites for executives, and clearly more of a prerequisite for women than for men, it suggests possible dangers and sources of problems. The first obvious problem is that the chance for coronary heart disease is multiplied. Preliminary research indicates that coronary disease tends to manifest itself as stroke in women rather than the myocardial infarction (heart attack) more common among men. Type A women tend to smoke more, drink more coffee, and exercise less, since they don't see exercise as a clearly productive activity. If they do exercise, they do so obsessively, thereby losing the benefits of relaxation.

Type A female executives, I have found, have a much higher probability of being divorced when compared to their male counterparts or to non-Type A women. When they are divorced, there is a high probability that they are also mothers and have custody of their child or children. Caring for children as a single parent, on top of a demanding managerial job in a pressure-cooker environment, places yet another source of stress on these women. Their male counterparts tend to be either single or married; if they are divorced fathers, the odds are great that they do not have custody of their children.

There are other expected problems more directly related to the workplace that tend to accompany Type A behavior and that affect both men and women:

1. *You have a tendency to overplan each day,* which usually results in not accomplishing everything you would like in a given period. Consequently, you are always behind in your self-imposed schedule of unrealistic goals, and the overscheduling creates a chronic sense of time urgency. Type A people simply try to accomplish too much in the time allotted. Even if it were possible to accomplish everything in a given day, you would then go on to plan additional activities and rush yourselves even more. If you overplan your days, it may be because you feel your success is the result of being able to accomplish things faster than other people do. Since haste

does not equal quality, however, your success may very well be in spite of, not because of, this characteristic.

2. *You have excessive competitive drive*, going beyond healthy competition and bordering on a compulsiveness to view everything as a challenge or competitive match. This carries over from business encounters to personal and social activities. You are concerned with numbers and quantity of output. The Type A competitive spirit, which forces you to compare your performance to that of others in virtually all aspects of life, creates a constant restlessness and feeling of discontent. Always focusing on your next goal, you cannot be happy with accomplishments already achieved. Winning becomes an end in itself. Although you usually claim to be motivated by the *challenge* to win, if you don't win, often, there is no enjoyment or pride in doing the activity itself.

3. *You are impatient with delays or interruptions.* Type A people have little patience with someone they feel is doing a job too slowly. Regardless of whether it is your responsibility to oversee that person's work, you will either interrupt to demonstrate a faster method or will look on with exasperation. Type As tend to be overly critical of the way other people do their work, especially when they see a more efficient way of getting the job done. This impatience carries over to life outside the workplace; you would like most things to operate at a fast clip. Even when you go out socially, you will hurry the pace of conversation or finish a sentence for another person. When you don't finish the sentence, you may find yourself watching the mouth of the person speaking to you. The second the mouth stops moving, you start talking. This characteristic is known as *latency response*: the gap of silence between one person's completion of a verbal message and the other person's response. As a Type A, you will tend to create short latency responses in your conversations.

Type As also tend to be *polyphasic* thinkers; they think along two lines simultaneously. While you listen to what others are trying to say, you may mentally be rehearsing your response at the same time. If you are involved in conversations, they can become monologues, resembling one-sided debates. Polyphasic thinking can also involve reading a newspaper while talking on the telephone, watching television while eating, or reading a magazine at the dinner table. This type of thinking can also be a liability in conceptualizing, because polyphasic thinkers tend to focus on the here and now rather than on more general possibilities for the future. In other words, it is more difficult to think conceptually when juggling multiple thoughts. Conceptual thinking is required of successful managers, since it is the means to accomplish long-term, strategic planning.

4. *You feel a chronic sense of time urgency.* You might claim this urgency is a function of your job, but very often you are attracted to the specific positions that place you in this time bind. Type As are always trying to accomplish more and more in less and less time. You create a continual conflict within yourself and often feel you are running on a treadmill that you cannot stop. Time pressures are a continual part of the Type A's life, and it may seem as though you live by the stop watch. Life becomes a daily rat race.

5. *You have an inability to relax without feeling guilt.* Even in their leisure activities, Type A individuals seldom relax. It is hard for you to refrain from thinking or talking about your work or the things that interest you. Perhaps because of some unresolved underlying guilt or feelings of inadequacy, you tend to overplan or overschedule your leisure activities to the point where your social life becomes burdensome. A classic Type A would find it very difficult to go to a quiet island for a week and lie on the beach all day, every day.

Which to Change: Corporate Gender or Individual Behavior?

We cannot easily change the competitive, achievement-oriented culture that keeps the corporate environment very friendly to and supportive of Type A behavior. In fact, we now realize that changing an organization's culture (and its gender) is extremely difficult, not always desirable, and perhaps unnecessary.

On the one hand, this organizational breeding of Type As can be attributed to selection, recruitment, and promotion systems determined in large part by the organization's culture. This culture, in turn, is almost always developed by men. On the other hand, if this culture is the ticket to an organization's success, perhaps we should not tamper with it but should instead manage the symptoms that may evolve from it. Masculine cultures are not bad in themselves; this way of describing the process simply helps us in further understanding organizational dynamics. In some cases the process may be appropriate in its ability to generate a driven, frenzied level of motivation; in others it may be inappropriate, if it drives people to leave or burns them out. Keep in mind, however, that significantly changing a corporation's culture within a short period of time is often out of the question. There is simply too much *history* involved, too strong an inertia.

We are then faced with changing someone from being a Type A and moving them in the direction of a Type B; this can also be a task of herculean proportions. Unless they have had serious health consequences as a result of their behavior pattern, Type As will not only deny that they have a problem but will attribute their success to this behavior.

The following are a sample of some strategies being used by practitioners to help Type A individuals who are motivated to change to a less frenetic life-style.[9]

Positive reinforcement methods can be helpful where the Type A business person can schedule fewer people to meet and less work to do in a given period of time, or shorten the time allotted for various business activities. You can design frequent "free periods" to devote to such "difficult" activities as daydreaming, reflecting on past memories, or finishing a pet project. You can set up a schedule where, for example, you reward yourself for meeting with someone for an hour who truly enhances your life by buying a special dessert or taking some time to read your favorite magazine. This reward would immediately be followed by a shorter session (half an hour) with someone who tends to elicit your Type A behavior: competitive feelings, hostility, impatience. Scheduled nonbusiness lunch hours can also be reinforcing if taken in settings that don't cue Type A behavior: taking a walk in the park or browsing through a bookstore.

Avoidance responding uses techniques that also tend to help. This category includes steps like not wearing a watch or having a clock in the office. Timepieces generate feelings of being in a hurry, of being late, of being overcommitted, and of being overwhelmed. Similarly, you can instruct your secretary not to interrupt you when you are with another person or engaged in some other activity. The secretary can also engineer incoming phone calls so that they do not register in your office. A ringing telephone constitutes another form of interruption and tends to act as a cue to hurry up.

Attempt to do only one thing at a time. While waiting for a phone call to go through, instead of trying to accomplish a second or third task, choose instead to drop your pen and look out the window or at a soothing picture to avoid having to do something in the waiting time. When you feel yourself becoming frustrated by not completing all the work you have scheduled in a given day, ask yourself, "Ten years from now, who will know or care?"

Another set of strategies are known as *response cost techniques*. These involve drills for changing your Type A behavior. For example, whenever you catch yourself speeding up your car to get through a yellow light at an intersection, penalize yourself immediately by turning to the right at the next corner. Circle the block and drive up to the same corner and the same signal light again. After penalizing yourself like this, you might find that you do the same thing a second time, but probably not a third. There are other response cost techniques which can be engineered within your job.

In conjunction with these methods, relaxation procedures are usually taught, along with *cognitive behavior modification*. Clearly, Type A behavior is directly related to the thoughts, attitudes, beliefs, and philosophies these people have regarding their relationship to the world around them. For example, one thought process might be, "I have to hurry and get everything done or people will think I'm not well organized." Another might be, "If I don't work at least fourteen hours a day, seven days a week, I won't be successful." Thoughts like these can be restructured so that they reflect a more realistic concept of self and the outcomes for which one is responsible.

Recognizing what you value and want out of life is the first step to modifying your behavior. Be responsive to the world around you. Remember that life is not a dress rehearsal—this is the real show. Adapt yourself to a reasonable pace; you will find yourself becoming more aware of your environment, and you will enjoy it more as well.

Reduce the tendency to think and speak rapidly by making a conscious attempt to hear what other people say. Curb the possibility of interrupting others by taking a slow, deep breath every time you feel the urge to finish someone's conversation.

Future Directions

The notion that corporations have a masculine culture provides one perspective for understanding the criteria organizations have established for executive women. If an organization is characterized as masculine, we can expect greater pressure on women to have a more masculine presence than would exist in a less masculine culture. Type A behavior seems to be one of the most powerful and acceptable mechanisms for a woman to meet this requirement. The irony, however, is that Type A drags along with it a number of other characteristics that may handicap effective managers.

Corporations survive in a competitive environment only at the pleasure of their marketplace, and satisfying the needs of the marketplace can be a grueling, aggressive, risky, and dominating experience. In turn, the more competitive the environment, the greater the requirement that the culture reflect characteristics like aggressiveness, competitiveness, ambitiousness, and strength.

The business world merely reflects the expectations we have traditionally ascribed to sex roles, but the culture is undergoing dynamic changes. Most companies would prefer to wait until societal attitudes change in favor of new roles for women before taking any action within their companies. Today, however, the business world does not have the luxury of waiting for social change to become institutionalized before changing the corporate culture. Corporate leaders are expected to create the change internally, which is easier said than done. A number of high-technology organizations, for example, have realized the need for nontraditional culture in order to maintain a constant stream of creative, innovative, and marketable ideas for products and their manufacture.

Studies have shown that, for numerous reasons, females have a lower self-concept than males and possibly a different orientation toward achievement as well.[10] In light of this, a company may not solve the problem of sex discrimination solely by eliminating unfair practices in pay, promotion, and opportunity. Women themselves may have to change, and the company that shrewdly recognizes the value of this major proportion of the work force will help them make the transition to a new role by taking these personality factors into consideration. Careful mentoring and coaching, combined with well-planned management development training, is one strategy for addressing the needs of women.

Equally important is the role played by the reward structures established in organizations. The formal structures provide for periodic evaluations, raises, bonuses, fringe benefits, promotions—all designed to be as objective and as fair as possible. But each organization also has its informal reward structure, its own subtle way of saying: "Do it *this* way, and you will be recognized and rewarded. If you do it another way, you'll be ignored or punished." The informal structure can leave much to be desired with respect to fairness, but nonetheless it is powerful and pervasive. Both forms reinforce not only *that* the job gets done but also *how* the job gets done. We constantly receive direct feedback and subtle cues from colleagues and superiors about how acceptable we are in the corporate environment.

Type A behavior, at least superficially, appears very productive and is often an underlying explanation for workaholism. People look busy, move fast, talk fast, and seem as though they are always working. As we have seen, however, in some cases the behavior is not necessarily productive but continues to be rewarded—and therefore reinforced—by the employer.

For women, the Type A imperative is further reinforced for yet another reason: it allows them to seem more like men, more worthy of being taken seriously. Perhaps as organizations, management practices, and the changing expectations of our culture evolve, women will be judged on more relevant criteria. Then, perhaps, the quality of their decisions and the skill with which they solve problems will override the degree to which they fit into a masculine culture.

Notes

1. "Against the Odds," *The New York Times Magazine*, January 6, 1985, p. 17.
2. A series of reports published in *The Wall Street Journal* from October 23 through November 1, 1985, conducted by the Gallup organization.

3. J. Wolff and N.C. Tarrand, "Male Mimicry by Human Females in Male Jobs," unpublished working paper, University of Virginia, Department of Biology, 1982.
4. S. Bem, "Psychological Androgyny," in Alice G. Sargent, ed., *Beyond Sex Roles* (St. Paul: West, 1977).
5. J.H. Howard, D.A. Cunningham, and P.A. Rechnitzer, "Work Patterns Associated with Type A Behavior: A Managerial Population," *Human Relations 30,* no. 9 (1977):825–836.
6. For additional discussion of this idea, see M. Matteson and J. Ivancevich, *Managing Job Stress and Health* (New York: The Free Press, 1982).
7. W.H. Jones, M.E. Chernovetz, and R.O. Hansson, "The Enigma of Androgyny: Differential Implications for Males and Females?" *Journal of Consulting and Clinical Psychology 46* (1978):298–313.
8. M.J. Davidson and C.L. Cooper, "Type A Coronary-Prone Behavior in the Work Environment," *Journal of Occupational Medicine 22* (1980):462–470.
9. For additional information, see, M. Friedman and D. Ulmer, *Treating Type A Behavior—and Your Heart* (New York: Knopf, 1984).
10. D.R. Kaufman, *Achievement and Women* (New York: The Free Press, 1982).

References

Baucom, D.H. 1980. "Independent CPI Masculinity and Feminity Scores." *Journal of Personality Assessment 44:*262–271.

Baucom, D.H. 1983. "Sex Role Identity and the Decision to Regain Control among Women: A Learned Helplessness Investigation." *Journal of Personality and Social Psychology 44:*334–343.

Berzins, J.I.; Welling, M.A.; and Wetter, R.E. 1976. "Androgynous vs. Traditional Sex Roles and the Interpersonal Behavior Circle," Paper presented at the annual meeting of the American Psychological Association, Washington, D.C.

Berzins, J.I.; Welling, M.A.; and Wetter, R.E. 1978. "A New Measure of Psychological Androgyny Based on the Personality Research Form." *Journal of Consulting and Clinical Psychology 46:*126–138.

Kanter, R.M. 1977. *Men and Women of the Corporation.* New York: Basic Books.

Lipton, M. 1985. "Masculinity and Management: Type A Behavior and the Corporation." *Organizational Development Journal 3,* no. 1 (Spring).

Moore, W. 1962. *The Conduct of the Corporation.* New York: Random House.

Sargent, A.G. 1983. *The Androgynous Manager.* New York: Amacom.

Schein, V.E. 1973. "The Relationship between Sex Role Stereotypes and Requisite Management Characteristics." *Journal of Applied Psychology 57:*95–100.

12
Mastering Change: The Skills We Need

Rosabeth Moss Kanter

M any professionals and popular writers concerned with developing women for management positions have tended to provide lists of rather inflexible rules and formulas—how to dress, how to get a mentor, how to play office politics—even though there is no evidence that these are actually crucial for success. Instead, we need to focus on what does make a difference in today's business environment: how to make a contribution to the organization's success. Increasingly, this involves skills in innovation and change.

For a long time, those of us writing about developing women seemed to act as though the organizational settings in which women were being developed were static, and nothing was changing. Thus the only important thing was the career path and how to get on that trajectory. But even if that static view was correct for the kind of corporation I studied in the early 1970s for *Men and Women of the Corporation*, it is no longer true in any institution in this society, in any sector.

Organizations are not standing still. There are increased competitive pressures in every environment, in every sector—in part because of the global economy and problems in our own economy, and in part because of intensified competition among and between industries, regardless of what those industries are. The educational business certainly is highly competitive now for students; so is nearly every other sector, not just what we call mainstream American industry. In fact, the most brutally aggressive talk I have heard recently about cut-throat competition and strategic positioning and competitive advantage was given by the managers and the head of nursing at a nonprofit hospital chain in Virginia.

There is no sector of U.S. society that is not concerned now with being more competitive in an era in which there are a constant set of problems, and demand and change requirements. The need for new and better solutions, the need for new and improved operations— whether that consists of new products, new services, new ways of organizing to deliver the products or the services better, new marketing techniques, new budgeting systems—makes *change* the central issue today.

Thus developing women, or any people, to be successful in today's environment involves teaching them not only how to cope with change and how to make sure their skills do not become obsolete, but also how to *lead change productively and positively.* The people I call *change masters*, people who are adept at the art of anticipating the need for change and leading it, hold the keys to success in today's environment.

I hope that the era in which people can rise in organizations simply because of political connections (like playing golf with the boss) is over. It is no accident that in the 1970s we focused so much intellectual attention on the politics of organization, because it *did* see that in a static environment, particularly a large organization, keeping one's nose clean and having a mentor or a sponsor and being well connected could make the difference in who rose in the pyramid. In today's environment, those purely political factors give way to others. Certainly relationships and connections and political alliances make a difference, but increasingly it is the ability to envision and lead something new that makes a difference. Thus the pressures of this era may finally create an organizatioal environment in which competence wlil dominate over politics, because organizations cannot afford to ignore competence when they are under competitive pressure.

If this is a very positive and promising era for women's career achievement, it is also one that demands a new and different kind of skill, not the ones emphasized as developers have reflected on an organizational environment that was considered more static, more stable, more steady-state.

I discovered the change master skills by researching hundreds of managers across more than a half dozen industries for my book *The Change Masters*. By now, the research has been replicated on about a dozen major organizations and several hundred more managers. The findings hold across both men and women; there seem to be few if any sex differences in the need for, existence of, or use of the skills. Although the data base has many fewer women than men represented at the levels that were the cutoff points for inclusion in the study, those women who had managed to reach the appropriate management levels actually outperformed the men in their ability to lead innovation. Perhaps the extra competence it took for the women to move into those male-dominated ranks in the first place stood them in very good stead.

The skills that make up my model are thus considered to be universal and to some extent learnable and teachable. I will put the "change master" skills in two categories: first, the personal or individual skills, and then the interpersonal ones connected to the way the person manages others.

Kaleidoscope Thinking

The first essential skill is a style of thinking, or a way of approaching the world, which I have come to call *kaleidoscope thinking*. The metaphor of a kaleidoscope is a good way of capturing exactly what innovators, or leaders of change, do. A kaleidoscope is a device for seeing patterns. It takes a set of fragments and forms them into a pattern. But when it is twisted, shaken, or approached from a new angle, the exact same fragments form an entirely different pattern. Kaleidoscope thinking, then, involves taking an existing array of data or existing array of phenomena or existing array of assumptions, and being able to twist them, shake them, look at them upside down or from another angle—from a new direction—permitting an entirely new set of actions to take place.

Change masters, or the leaders of change, are not necessarily more creative than other people, but they are more willing to move outside of received wisdom, to approach problems from new angles.

This is a classic finding in the history of any kind of innovation—that the old beliefs must be challenged before change can occur. A large proportion of important innovations are brought about by people who step outside conventional categories or conventional assumptions. They are often *not* the experts or the specialists—although for years women have been educated to be experts and specialists. Instead, the boundary crossers or generalists who know how to move across fields or across sectors, who know how to move outside what everybody else is looking at, are the leaders in a changing organization (or an organization in need of change). Experts and specialists tend to look at the world through a microscope, not a kaleidoscope. They become too detail-conscious. They get to know their field, and the way things have always been done in the past, so well that it becomes impossible for them to see any other options. Experts and specialists are often doomed to repeat the past because of their microscopic vision. The common traditional complaint about women-as-managers—that they were too-detail conscious—reflects the microscope problem.

Kaleidoscope thinking begins with experience outside one's own field or department. Moving outside for broadened perspectives was common in the history of every innovation I studied. A woman change master at a computer company began an important project this way. When she got her assignment, the first thing she did was leave her area and roam around the rest of the organization, talking it over with nearly everyone she could find, regardless of field, looking for new angles, new perspectives, new ways to approach it so that what she could bring back would be new and creative. She did not start with what other people could bring her; she crossed boundaries to do that.

This is how many important changes have been seeded. One example is the invention of frozen vegetables. Frozen vegetables were invented by Clarence Birdseye, who had a produce business at the turn of the century. The conventional wisdom of his time, like that of our own time, held that the best way to run a business (or a department) was to "mind the store"—one's field and only one's field, as in the microscope image: watch, control, and get better and better at knowing just one thing. But Birdseye was an adventurer, and so, like many change masters, he wandered away from the problem, he wandered outside his territory, and he went on expeditions. On one of his adventure trips, fur-trapping in Labrador, he discovered the phenomenon that fish caught in ice could be eaten much later. He brought that idea back and transformed his business from a local produce store to the beginnings of national distribution. The rest is history.

Organizations that seek innovation ought to learn from this kind of experience: allow people to move outside the orthodoxy of an area, to mix and match, to shake up assumptions.

One chief executive believed that this kind of thinking was so important to his organization's success in a high-tech field (though not in computers), that he staged a highly imaginative top management meeting. He took his top fifty officers to a resort to hold their annual financial planning meeting. Although it started out just like their usual meetings, he wanted this year to be different. He was concerned that they were getting stuck in a rut, and that he was not getting much creative thinking, although his company needed innovation for survival. He made the point symbolically. Halfway through his talk, the meeting was suddenly interrupted by a set of men dressed as prison guards, who burst into the room, grabbed everybody there, and took them out to a set of waiting helicopters, which flew them off to a second meeting site. The executive said: "Now we'll begin again, and we'll bury all the thinking we were doing in the last meeting, and we'll approach everything from a new angle. I want new thinking out of you." He continued to punctuate the meeting with a set of surprises, like a parade of elephants on the beach. First there was a small elephant, with the natural financial goal painted on its side. Then along came a bigger elephant with a bigger number, and then a huge elephant with a huge number, and he said: "Go for it! Stretch your thinking!" The symbolism of the whole meeting was to stretch, move outside, challenge assumptions, twist that kaleidoscope.

In light of these examples, I wonder whether there has been too much emphasis on teaching women to conform, to fit into the system. Certainly that suits conservative organizations in conservative times. But now that innovation and creativity are necessary, it is time to reemphasize novel ways of thinking. Women may have an edge precisely because they *haven't* been brought up all those years to be somebody fitting exactly into the system. Perhaps developers have to tap that and make it productive for the organization. As "outsiders," perhaps women can be more objective in analyzing situations—a real plus for the organization.

So kaleidoscope thinking was the first thing I found to be true of the people who led innovations or accomplished productive changes.

Communicating Visions

The second conclusion I drew about change masters' individual skills was their ability to articulate and communicate *visions*. New and creative ideas and better ways to do things come not from *systems* but from *people*. People leading other people in untried directions are the true shapers of change. So behind every change, every innovation, every development project, there must be somebody with a vision who has been able to communicate and sell that vision to somebody else (even when the change begins with an assignmeent, not a self-directed initiative).

Although *innovation* is a very positive term, it is important to remember that any *particular* innovation is only positive in retrospect, *after* it has worked. Before that—because change by definition is something no one has seen yet (despite models that may exist elsewhere)—it has to be taken at least partially on faith. For example, why a continuing education program now? Why use funds to develop a new product when there are so many already on the market that need support? Why take the risk of decentralizing the accounting office?

In short, unless there is somebody behind the idea willing to take the risk of speaking up for it, the idea will disappear. In fact, I argue that one reason that there is so little change in most traditional bureaucratic organizations is that they have conditioned out of people the willingness to stand up for a new idea. Instead, people learn to back off at the first sign that somebody might disapprove.

This second change master skill can be called *leadership*. Martin Luther King's famous speech in the 1963 march on Washington articulated this as "I have a dream." He didn't say: "I have a few ideas; there seem to be some problems out there. Maybe if we set up a few committees, something will happen." But when I see how many people present their ideas in just this sort of well-if-you-don't-like-it-that's-all-right way, I can understand why they are not necessarily effective in getting things done. Innovation, change, new projects—even the conservative and apparently desirable ones—require that somebody put him- or herself behind it and push, especially when things get difficult, as they always do when change is involved. This kind of leadership involves communication plus conviction.

Thus developers should be teaching women to learn about and come to trust their own instincts, to have high enough self-esteem and self-regard to believe in their own visions, and to be willing to convey them as something important that other people should be willing to pay attention to.

Persistence

The third personal skill is related to having a vision. Leaders of innovation persist in an idea; they keep at it. When I examined the difference between the success and failure in change projects or development efforts, I found that one major difference was simply *time*—staying with it long enough to make it work.

To some extent, *everything* looks like a failure in the middle. There is a point or points in the history of every project, every effort, when discouragements mount and the temptation to stop is great. But pulling out at that moment automatically equals failure. There is nothing to show for the effort yet. The inevitable problems, roadblocks, and low spots when enthusiasm wanes prevent you from getting to a return on the investment of time and resources. Without persistence at that point, important changes, important new projects will never happen.

In large organizations the number of roadblocks and low points can seem infinite. Particularly when something new is being tried, there are not only all the technical details of how the new program is going to work, but also all the political difficulties of handling the critics. Critics are more likely to surface in the middle than at the beginning because the project has become a little more of a threat. There is little incentive for the critics to tie up political capital by challenging the project until it looks as though it is actually going to happen. This is a reality of organizational life.

At one major consumer products company, this phenomenon was demonstrated very well to me. They have a product that's now on our supermarket shelves, which to them is now a big success. But when this project was in the development stage, it was known as "Project Lazarus" because it rose from the dead so many times. Four times, people at higher levels tried to kill it off, and four times the people working on it came back and fought for it, argued for it, provided justification and evidence for why it should continue: "Just give us a little more time; we need a little more time. We know we can make it work." Every organization has examples like this one. If the team had stopped, the effort would have been a total loss. But arguing for the additional time and money, and confronting the critics, turned a potential failure into a success.

Unless people are encouraged to persist, meaningful accomplishments are difficult to achieve. Developers must teach women to tolerate difficulties and become comfortable with the longer time frame it takes to make significant things happen (and not to identify *personally* with the setbacks that will occur along the way).

Coalition Building

In addition to the personal skills of change masters, there are also interpersonal and organizational skills. The first of these is coalition building. At the point where there is a creative idea, with someone with a vision behind it willing to persist, it still has to be sold to other people in the organization in order to be implemented. Although the literature on organizational politics has emphasized one-on-one relationship building, my research moves the emphasis to the coalition. What makes people effective in organizations is the ability to create a whole set of backers and supporters, specifically for innovative activities, which helps lend the power necessary to get those activities to happen. In this sense an entrepreneur inside a corporation is just like an entrepreneur outside: they have to find the bankers, the people who will provide the funds; they have to find the information sources; and they have to find the key sources of legitimacy and support who will put their names on the letterhead or will champion the project to other powerholders.

Multiple sponsors and multiple backers make the difference, not just one. An attractive young woman who now holds one of the top six positions in a U.S. corporation began as assistant to the chairman and was subjected to many innuendoes about their relationship. But she proved to be a highly effective change master in her organization, responsible for many successful new projects, because she is a superb coalition builder, drawing hardly at all on her relationship with the CEO. She brings others into projects; she works with peers and people below to make them feel included. She creates multiple relationships and teams around her of people who have a stake in each project and are going to get something out of it. Because of her coalition-building skills, she led successful change projects that in turn brought her recognition and early promotions. She is a visible example that the Mary Cunningham tragedy does not have to happen to other women.

Coalitions are especially important where change is needed, because innovation, or new projects or new developments, generally involve going outside already existing organizational sources of power. My research found that managers who wanted to innovate, or try something new, almost invariably needed more resources, information, and support than they had. They often needed money above and beyond their budget (though sometimes not much) because usually their budget was for routine, ongoing things they were doing; if they wanted to do something new, they had to find extra funds. They also needed higher levels of support, because innovations sometimes interfere with other things going on in an organization. Change is often resisted because it can be a nuisance and an interference; it requires other people to stop what they are doing or redirect their thinking. And new efforts also tend to require more information, more data, new sources of knowledge. Thus the change masters I studied *had* to build a coalition in order to find the people who should be the backers or power sources to provide information, support, and resources for their projects.

Coalition building not only attracts needed power to a project, it also tends to help guarantee success. Once others are brought in and contribute their money or their support to a project, they also have a stake in making it work. As a result, the innovator is not out there all by herself, trying to convince a reluctant organization to do something. There are now other people to serve as cheerleaders.

This process of coalition building is so well known in some of the high-tech companies in my research that they have invented their own language around it. They call the whole process one of getting *buy-in* or generating wider ownership of a project from key supporters. First is a low-key step of gathering intelligence and planting seeds—just finding out where people stand and leaving behind a germ of the idea to let it blossom so it becomes familiar. Then the serious business of coalition building begins in the process they call *tin-cupping*. The manager, symbolically, takes his or her "tin cup" in hand and walks around the organization, "begging" for involvement, seeing who has a little bit to chip in, who has a few spare budget dollars to invest, who has a staff member to lend, who will be on the advisory committee, or who has key data. In the process of tin-cupping, two very important organizational functions take place that guard against failures. (In high-tech firms, the only failures at innovation that I saw occurred where the manager thought he or she already had so much power that coalition building was unnecessary.) One is the "horse trading" required. For everything that is dropped into the tin cup, people have to feel that they get something back. Thus one person's project has to be translated into something of wider benefit around the organization—which helps ensure that it will work because it has support. And in the course of tin-cupping, an innovator also gets a "sanity check"—feedback from older and wiser heads helping reshape the idea to make it more workable.

Coalition building, therefore, not only provides a personal or political advantage but is also a very important process for making sure the ideas that do get developed have merit and wider support. It is a form of peer control, a way of screening out bad or nonimplementable ideas. For this reason, at one computer company, top management is more likely to provide large allocations for ideas that come with a coalition already formed around them.

Working through Teams

Once a group of supporters has been generated, it's time to get down to the actual project work. Now the next interpersonal/organizational skill comes into play: the ability to build a working team to carry out the idea.

Very few ideas, very few projects of any significance, are implemented by one person alone; it generally takes other people helping to make it happen, whether they are assistants, subordinates, a staff, or a special project team or task force of peers assembled just for this effort. But regardless of who the people are, it is crucial that they feel like a *team* in order to make an idea work.

My research documents the relationship between participative management and innovation—providing hard evidence for the importance of participative management when change is involved, even if it is not necessary for managing the routine. Full involvement turns out to be crucial when the issue is change. For a routine operation, where everybody knows what he or she is doing, high involvement and high commitment are less crucial. But change requires above-and-beyond effort on the part of all the people involved. It requires their creativity and their commitment. Without this extra effort, those trying to make something significant happen in an organization, and who are dependent on other people's help to get that done, find the help difficult to get. People will find other priorities, they'll be late with reports. Everybody in an organization has at least one form of power—the pocket veto. Even without directly challenging an idea, all they have to do is sit on it for a while, put it in their pockets, not respond, find other priorities, be late with reports—and the change effort will be stalled. Loss of momentum occurs when other people are not motivated to do their part.

The history of the development of a new computer at Data General illustrates the process of team building very well. Tom West, the middle manager behind this development team, worked very hard to create a self-conscious sense of *team*—team play, ownership, and identification. He led young engineers just out of school to perform engineering miracles—record-time achievements that nobody had predicted. Their intense sense of ownership came from a team identity, symbolized by names and by many occasions for fun together. They were given full responsibility and were kept fully informed. They were given plenty of room to make mistakes. West, the manager, supported by two assistants, did not impose his ideas on the team. Indeed, when he had solutions to problems, he sometimes went to the lab late at night and left them behind on slips of paper for people to find in the morning—without knowing how they got there. Thus he created an atmosphere in which people felt autonomous and in control, and consequently felt incredibly dedicated and committed to the project.

Those are the skills essential for managing change teams—skills women have just as men do.

Sharing the Credit

Finally, bringing innovation full circle, the last thing that people who lead changes must do involves sharing the credit and recognition—making everyone a hero. Instead of simply taking individual credit, change masters make sure that everyone who works on their effort is rewarded.

This behavior tends to come back to the benefit of the person who is leading the change. I saw this dramatically illustrated in an insurance company. A manager had led a series of employee involvement projects that dramatically improved productivity in his region and had an impact on the insurance company's profits. At bonus time, his management was going to reward him with a big bonus. He went to his management and asked if he could have bonus money for the people below who had also contributed to his efforts. The company, unfortunately, turned him down. So he took several thousand dollars from his own pocket, collected similar sums from the people around him, and made up his own bonus pool for everyone down to the clerical level who had contributed. That not only made people feel that their last effort was rewarded, but also got them excited about being part of the next organizational improvement. Change became a great opportunity rather than a threat.

For many people, these kinds of projects—new developments, change, innovation—are the most significant things they feel they have ever done in their work lives. My research found people who had spent thirty years in a big bureaucracy but said that the development task force they'd been on for the last six months was the only thing they were excited by and the only thing they would be remembered for—their mark on the organization. Change, the development of something new, unleashes people's creative energy;

It is exhilarating in a way that routine work isn't. Giving people the opportunity for innovation and also recognizing them for it are ways of meeting both organizational and individual needs.

Again, women historically have learned good nurturing behavior and can give good positive feedback.

The Organization's Contribution to Change Mastery

Although the change masters I studied had these six skills in common, they were also influenced by the encouragement or discouragement they received from their organizations. We need to focus not on the individual alone, but on the individual in context.

My research documented that there were more people able to act as change masters in certain kinds of environments. Some kinds of environments encourage people to rise above themselves, to become more creative, to become better able to make connections and build coalitions than others. This is likelier in organizations where jobs are defined in broad rather than narrow terms, where people are given grand goals to shoot for rather than narrow definitions of exactly what to do each day. They tend to be places organized around smaller departments or smaller units or smaller teams, where people can have a whole thing to grasp—the equivalent of managing their own business or managing their own part of the organization.

They tend to be places that have what I call the *culture of pride.* A message is sent that says, "We're all winners; people around me value me, people here are creative and talented and able to achieve." The message comes from the sheer amount of money spent on developing and training people, on attending to their needs. It comes from abundant praise and recognition systems.

Organizations also encourage change mastery by making information easy to get, so that people communicate across departments, across areas, across boundaries, and get to know each other. In high innovation settings there is abundant networking. The high-innovation, progressive companies in my research were, in fact, more likely to have active women's networks (formal or informal), because the very idea of relationships-building across areas is much more common in places where change is encouraged, where management wants people to be reaching out and reaching beyond—forming coalitions and making things happen. Finally, supportive environments make resources easier to get by setting aside uncommitted funds people can use for projects of their own initiative.

In short, change masters flourish in a kind of culture and structure that I call *integrative*—where people pull together instead of pulling apart. People are not rigidly divided on the basis of department or status or level or sex, and the organization is less category-conscious; what is important is getting things done, not who does them. There is a sense of teamwork, a knowledge of the whole; there is an ability to reach out and embrace more of the organization.

The opposite, the kinds of places that stifle and discourage innovations and inhibit women's development, resemble the company I described in *Men and Women of the Corporation*. I call these organizations *segmentalist* because they divide things into segments, into categories, into compartments, and keep them as far apart as possible. Departments fail to communicate with other levels. Organizations that are segmentalist compartmentalize experience and do not allow people to reach beyond the givens of their job to do more. They encourage microscopic thinking: detail-conscious, oriented toward specialties, oriented toward the status quo. they are places in which departments compete with each other, forgetting that the *whole* organization has to survive. I found a sobering number of examples of this territory-defending behavior in older, more traditional organizations, where powerlessness reigned.

The organizational context counts. We can do wonderful things for women, motivate them, and teach them how to be leaders. But if they then go to work in places that do not allow the new skills to be expressed, they are wasted. We must therefore enlarge the focus from developing individuals to developing new-style organizations better suited to today's highly competitive, change-demanding environment.

About the Contributors

Lynda L. Moore is an assistant professor of management at Simmons College in Boston, Massachusetts, where she teaches courses in behavioral implications for women in management, organizational behavior, and human resource management. She has taught women at every level, from undergraduate students to executives.

Her research and writing have focused on the career development of women in management. She has presented papers and led seminars in numerous professional meetings. Dr. Moore is a consultant to both for-profit and not-for-profit organizations in the area of human resource management, specializing in women in management. She belongs to many professional organizations and holds several national offices in organizations dedicated to the professional development of women. She is executive director of the Institute for Women and Organizations. Her doctorate is from the University of Massachusetts.

Lisa M. Amoss is adjunct professor of human resources management at the A.B. Freeman School of Business, Tulane University. She is also president of A.B.T. Associates, a management consulting firm. Ms. Amoss has been a management consultant to corporations, not-for-profit organizations, and entrepreneurial ventures since 1975. She specializes in working with female managers and women-owned businesses.

Lee Anne Bell is co-founder of Professional Development Associates, Inc., and assistant professor of education at the State University of New York at New Paltz. She teaches graduate courses in staff development, group dynamics, and organizational change. She is currently working on a grant to develop curricula to help undergraduate women overcome the imposter syndrome.

Dr. Bell consults with educational, government, and human service organizations on leadership, decision making, problem solving, team building, and communication. She is currently developing leadership models for women and minority managers and has co-authored a book on enhancing intergroup relations.

Dr. Bell received an Ed.D. from the University of Massachusetts at Amherst, an M.Ed. from the University of Hartford, and a B.A. from Indiana University at Bloomington.

Nicholas J. Beutell is director, Division of Research, and associate professor of management in the W. Paul Stillman School of Business, Seton Hall University. He received his Ph.D. in human resource management from Stevens Institute of Technology.

James G. Clawson is an associate professor at the Colgate Darden Graduate School of Business Administration at the University of Virginia. He received an A.B. from Stanford, an M.B.A. from Brigham Young University, and a D.B.A. from the Harvard Business School. His research interests focus on the relationship between individuals and organizations, most currently on career management from both perspectives. His writings have appeared in *Business Horizons, Exchange*, and the *Training and Development Journal*. His book *Self Assessment and Career Development* was published in 1985. He consults with a number of organizations on human resource management systems and management development. Professor Clawson teaches courses in organizational behavior, organization design, leadership and intergroup conflict, and self-assessment and career development.

Marcy Crary is an assistant professor of management at Bentley College. She earned her Ph.D. from Case Western Reserve University following a B.A. from Harvard. Her current research focuses on adult development and male-female relations at work. Her work appears in *The Organizational Behavior Teaching Review*. She has consulted for both public- and private-sector organizations in areas related to quality of work life and organizational effectiveness. Professor Crary teaches courses in organizational behavior, group dynamics, interpersonal relations, women in organizations, and organizational structure and design.

Roderick W. Gilkey is a clinical psychologist who specializes in the experiences and problems of business executives. He has degrees from Harvard and the University of Michigan, and is currently on the faculty of Emory University. Previously, he was on the faculties of the Amos Tuck School of Business Administration and Dartmouth Medical School.

His teaching experience has spanned the range from negotiation and applied psychology to various clinical topics. His consulting activities have included working with executives and their families, helping professionals make career choices, and diagnosing interpersonal problems within organizations. Dr. Gilkey is the author of articles and professional papers in the clinical and management fields.

Leonard Greenhalgh is associate professor at the Amos Tuck School of Business Administration at Dartmouth College. He has an MBA, and a Ph.D. degree in organizational behavior from Cornell University. His business experience includes managing a department in a large multinational, founding and operating a small corporation, working full time as a management consultant, and running a research operation of twenty-five employees.

His teaching experience includes negotiation, applied psychology, organizational behavior, human resource management, and numerous executive development programs. He has written two books and more than sixty professional papers. His research has concentrated on negotiation and conflict resolution, the organizational careers of professionals, and declining organizations.

Jeffrey H. Greenhaus is professor of management in the Department of Management and Organizational Sciences, Drexel University. He holds a B.A. degree from Hofstra University and a Ph.D. in industrial-organizational psychology from New York University.

Joanna Henderson has worked in both the corporate and academic worlds. She was the director of career planning and placement at

Wheaton College after directing the off-campus internship program at Dartmouth College for several years. She held faculty appointments in the education departments at both of these institutions.

On the corporate side, she was the director of professional recruiting at DRI/McGraw Hill before moving into a marketing position within that company. Most recently she was the district manager in McGraw Hill's Boston office for *Electronics Week*.

She holds a doctorate in the sociology of education from the University of Massachusetts at Amherst and a master's degree in sociology from Dartmouth.

She has written widely on the subject of women and their careers and is currently writing full time.

Natasha Josefowitz is an adjunct professor of the College of Human Services, San Diego State University, and has taught at their College of Business, at the Whittemore School of Business and Finance of the University of New Hampshire, and at Lausanne University in Switzerland.

She is the author of *Paths to Power,* a woman's guide from first job to top executive; *Is This Where I Was Going?,* a book of humorous verse; and *You're the Boss, Managing with Understanding and Effectiveness.* Dr. Josefowitz's articles have appeared in both academic journals and popular magazines.

She is a consultant to both industry and service organizations, has written a semimonthly management column, has her own weekly segment on public radio, and a monthly live question-and-answer section on television.

Rosabeth Moss Kanter is chairman of the board of Goodmeasure, Inc., an international management consulting firm specializing in strategies for innovation, productivity, and effective management of change.

She is the author of *The Change Masters: Innovations for Productivity in the American Corporation* and *Men and Women of the Corporation,* among other books, and of numerous articles in books and magazines. She is the Class of 1960 Professor at the Harvard Business School, the first holder of this new tenured full professorship dedicated to innovation and entrepreneurship. Dr. Kanter received her B.A. from Bryn Mawr College and her Ph.D. from the University of Michigan. She has held teaching appointments at Brandeis, Harvard, Yale, and the Massachusetts Institute of Technology.

Bonnie R. Kasten is a managing partner of Kasten Cramer, an entrepreneurial productivity consulting firm. She has consulted to over a hundred organizations and has trained over three thousand managers in complex negotiation strategy and influence skills.

Bonnie was a human resource manager in a Fortune 500 energy company and in an international training and development company. She has also been a college administrator. She is a graduate of the Columbia Executive Program in Human Resource Management, Arizona State University, and the University of South Dakota.

She is president of the Business Women's Network in Philadelphia, Pennsylvania, and a member of NTL Institute in Rosslyn, Virginia.

Reba L. Keele, Ph.D. (Purdue University), is an associate professor of organizational behavior in the Graduate School of Management at Brigham Young University. She just completed a nineteen-month leave in which she conceptualized, implemented, and managed the Center for Women's Health at Cottonwood Hospital Medical Center in Salt Lake City, Utah. She is a regent for the Utah System of Higher Education (serving on the executive committee and chairing the curriculum and rules committee) and a member of the Utah State Planning Committee of the American Council on Education National Identification Project.

She is one of forty-three young leaders chosen in 1985 as a W.K. Kellogg National Fellow, participating in a three-year program of leadership training and research. Her research is on relationships in career development, social support, and health care management. She is a member of the Academy of Management, the Consortium for Utah Women in Higher Education, and the American Management Association.

Kathy E. Kram is an assistant professor in the Department of Organizational Behavior at the Boston University School of Management. She has B.S. and M.S. degrees from the MIT Sloan School of Management and a Ph.D. from Yale University. Her primary research interests are in the areas of adult development and careers, male-female dynamics in organizations, ethical decision making in corporate life, and organizational change processes. She has articles in *Organizational Dynamics, The Academy of Management Journal, Organizational Behavior and Human Performance*, and *The Psychology of Women Quarterly*. Her book *Mentoring at Work* was published in 1985. She consults with private- and public-sector organizations on a variety of human resource management concerns. Professor Kram teaches courses in human behavior in organizations, leadership and group dynamics, self-assessment and careers, and organization development and change.

Jacqueline Landau is an assistant professor of organizational behavior at the A.B. Freeman School of Business, Tulane University. She received her Ph.D. from the New York State School of Industrial and Labor Relations, Cornell University. Her research focuses on career mobility and development. The research project she coordinated, on which this chapter is based, won the 1984 Southern College Placement Association Innovation and Research Award.

Mark Lipton is associate professor and chairman of the Management Department at the Graduate School of Management, New School for Social Research, in New York. He holds a Ph.D. from the School of Management at the University of Massachusetts/Amherst, where he also taught before joining the New School.

Currently, he also directs an innovative management development program sponsored by the New School and the Revson Foundation for select New York City government managers. He maintains a private consulting practice specializing in management and organization development, working with clients from both the corporate and government sectors.

Mark's research is now exploring a range of characteristics shared by successful female executives in high technology companies. He is also writing a book that will include and elaborate further on the concepts introduced in his chapter.

Betty Lou Marple is assistant dean, director of special programs at the Harvard Graduate School of Design. She has worked for men and women of all ages during a career that includes many years in higher education at Radcliffe College, Brandeis University, and Wellesley College, among others. She holds a Ph.D. in counseling psychology from Boston College, an MBA from Northeastern University, an M.Ed. from Harvard University, and a B.A. in economics from Vassar College. Her research interests are in the areas of management supervision and workplace climates.

Duncan Spelman is an assistant professor of management at Bentley College. He holds an A.B. degree from Princeton, an Ed.M. from Harvard, and a Ph.D. from Case Western Reserve University. His primary research interests include dual-career couples and male-female attraction at the workplace. He has written for *The Organizational Behavior Teaching Review* and *The Academy of Management Review*. His consulting activities have focused on a broad range of human resources issues and have included clients from business and industry, education, and the arts. Professor Spelman teaches courses in organizational behavior, interpersonal relations, and management.

Valerie E. Young is an Associate with New Perspectives, Inc., an Amherst, Massachusetts, consulting firm dedicated to helping individuals and organizations realize women's full career potential. In addition to working with organizations in both the public and private sectors to develop training and policies, she is widely known for her public seminars entitled "Imposters, Fakes and Frauds: A Career-Related Workshop for Women Who Doubt Their Competence."

Dr. Young is currently designing management training programs and organizational designs for increasing women's career potential. She is a frequent guest speaker at professional women's organizations and is the author of a paper entitled "Five Internal Barriers Blocking Women's Achievement."

Dr. Young received both her doctoral and master's degrees from the University of Massachusetts at Amherst in human relations and staff development.